STUDIES AND APPRECIATIONS

STUDIES AND
APPRECIATIONS

BY

LEWIS EDWARDS GATES

Essay Index Reprint Series

BOOKS FOR LIBRARIES PRESS
FREEPORT, NEW YORK

PR
99
.G3
1970

First Published 1900
Reprinted 1970

INTERNATIONAL STANDARD BOOK NUMBER:
0-8369-1927-0

LIBRARY OF CONGRESS CATALOG CARD NUMBER:
76-134079

PRINTED IN THE UNITED STATES OF AMERICA

CONTENTS

THE ROMANTIC MOVEMENT

THE era of modern life, in England as in France, dates from 1789. The nineteenth century began in the year in which the shock of the French Revolution went crisping over the nerves of the nations of Europe, stirred all men to novel thoughts and new moods, and startled them into fresh ways of envisaging life. If, however, the student of English literature wants a specifically literary and a national date for the beginning of the new era, the year 1800 offers itself as curiously apt; in that year appeared Wordsworth's Preface to the *Lyrical Ballads*, which as truly though not so consciously as Hugo's Preface to *Cromwell* nearly thirty years later, was the manifesto of a revolutionary movement. Wrong-headed as was Wordsworth's declaration that the Muse ought to speak with the burr of Cumberland peasants, and absurd as was the tangle of inconsistencies into which his acceptance of metre and his rejection of all other differences between prose and poetry betrayed him, yet even these parts of his Preface, because of their plea for veraciousness in poetry and their insistence on poetry as the *natural* idiom for deep

B   1

feeling, were essentially modern and were on the whole salutary in their influence; and as for the rest of the Preface, it stated doctrine after doctrine about the nature of poetry and the relations of poetry to life that for a quarter of a century the new age went on working out and illustrating, often, of course, in the persons of poets who were quite unaware of Wordsworth's programme. Poetry was no longer to be thought of as an ingenious stringing together of moral epigrams by clever craftsmen; it was to be the "spontaneous overflow of powerful feelings." The old doctrine that a poem gets its worth from the dignity of its subject was condemned; the poet's moods were to be the measure of all things; any subject from a primrose or a Cumberland beggar to man's longing for immortality might furnish forth the substance for a poem, providing it stirred the poet's heart sincerely and deeply. Above all, poetry was not to be regarded as a mere graceful pastime; it was to be reverenced as the one mode of utterance for the most intimate truths about man and nature that the human spirit can reach; it was to be exalted as "the first and last of all knowledge . . . immortal as the heart of man."'

One could hardly ask for a better account of the new spirit in literature — of the spirit that was to inform the best poetry and prose during the next twenty-five years — than Wordsworth's Preface offers. It specifies or suggests nearly all

the aspects of the complete renovation of literature which the new age was to accomplish, and
nearly all the varieties of new spiritual experience
which the men of the new dispensation were to
win and interpret.   In one of his letters, Keats
sums up life as a *soul-making* process.   "Call the
world if you please," he says, "'The Vale of Soul-
Making.'"   This may well stand as the legend
of the Romanticists.   They were the rediscoverers
of the soul; or, if one prefers the word that M.
Pellissier uses in describing the similar movement
in France, they were reasserters of the primacy of
the spirit.   Under this formula may be brought
whatever is most characteristic alike in the poetry
of Wordsworth, Coleridge, Scott, Byron, Shelley,
and Keats, and in the prose of Hazlitt, Lamb,
Leigh Hunt, and De Quincey.

To speak of Scott's poems and romances as having spiritual quality may seem fantastic.   Jenny
Lind used to say querulously of Scott that he did
no good to her soul; and Peacock's favourite jeer
at the Wizard of the North was that he was merely
a gigantic master of pantomime and harlequinade,
no end clever in engineering showy spectacles and
in decking out mock pageants in tinsel and stage-
finery, but a bungler in all that concerns the mind
and the heart.   Yet despite such jeers as these, it
may safely be asserted that the influence of Scott's
writings was in large measure a spiritual influence.
Scott quickened and fostered in the race a new

spiritual sense — the sense for its historical past;
he deepened and widened the national consciousness and made it include not merely its own passing phases, but also the earlier stages of thought
and of feeling, of custom, of belief, and of worship
through which in the Middle Ages it had worked
its way.   His Sir Brian de Bois-Guilbert and
Richard Cœur de Lion and Quentin Durward may
not have been either very minutely or very accu-
rately realized; yet their hopes and their longings
and their hates and their struggles, their passions
of pursuit and repulsion were with some degree of
faithfulness captured and portrayed and were thus
brought within the sympathetic appreciation of the
men of the early nineteenth century; and the various social forces of feudalism — these, too, with
their rhythms of aspiration and achievement, were
imaginatively reproduced and a vital sense of them
was conveyed into the minds and the hearts of the
new generation.   This meant the enrichment and
the deepening of consciousness, the infusion into
it of new colour, new variety, new elements of feeling, new sources of delight.   The eighteenth-century consciousness had been but a shallow affair.
It had contented itself in its typical state with such
ideas and feelings as a man of the world might need
at an assembly so as to chatter about the foibles or
follies of the town, or in a council-chamber for the
analysis of court intrigue or political manœu-
vring, or with such conceptions as at the utmost an

abstract thinker might in his closet discover and tabulate, — reasoning on prosaic experience with the help of mathematics and logic. The good folk of the eighteenth century were, above all, people of intellect who prided themselves on their rationality, who despised the insensate enthusiasm and the fatuous superstitions that the Middle Ages had revelled in, and who did their best to forget the Gothic absurdities of those Don-Quixote-like ancestors of theirs whose imaginations, as Swift put it, were perpetually astride on their reasons. The eighteenth century boasted of being an age of quite novel refinement and enlightenment: it purged itself of old prejudices, old beliefs, old passions; it concentrated itself on common-sense tasks both in practical life and in the life of the intellect; it scorned in actual life whatever could not be made to tally with its own somewhat ironical social instincts and in intellectual life whatever defied the rule of three or the sorites and the syllogism. Hence the beautiful clearness and also the impoverished simplicity of the experience of this century and of its literature. Against the shallowness of this purely intellectual and conventional life a mighty reaction began in the last half of the century, and Scott's work was one phase of the culmination of this reaction. Scott himself, it is true, had no new insight into what are technically called spiritual problems. He was no transcendentalist or "ideal-blind" enthusiast; he offered nothing either

in his poems or in his romances that could directly
help his readers into a surer relation toward the
mysterious powers of the spiritual world. But his
influence tended, with a decisiveness that we now
find it hard to realize, to break down the bounds
of the old-time, narrow, conventional, and purely
intellectual world in which the witty men of the
eighteenth century had lived and had tried to believe they were thriving. He touched the men of
his day into a vital sense of kinship with the men
of the Middle Ages — with the men of those "ages
of faith" wherein life was lived passionately and
imaginatively under haunted heavens. And so he
gave to his readers both a new belief in their
hearts and imaginations and a great mass of new
feelings and new sympathies. He made a potential gift to each of his readers of an individual past
of a thousand years of intense living.

Scott's vogue as a poet yielded to that of Byron,
and in Byron's verse the revolt against the commonplace, that in Scott had been only implicit,
became fiercely aggressive. In the interests of
individual freedom Byron quarrelled with life in a
twofold way; he assailed conventional prejudice
that held in check free play of feeling and action,
and that tried to compel every respectable person
to form himself on an eighteenth-century traditional pattern of rational correctness; and he went
still farther and arraigned the whole scheme of the
universe for not conspiring to minister obediently

to the needs of his craving egoism. If Scott had been chiefly decorative, Byron was above all things ethical, and his enormous popularity was due to the audacious moral challenge of his verse. He had the declamatory eloquence of the hustings which an English public readily understands; and as he harangued in somewhat garish rhetoric on "custom's falsest scale," and on "the fire and motion of the soul," described ornately the splendid carnal orgies of his Oriental heroes, and above all hinted darkly at his own mischances and misdeeds and hymned in triumphant rhythms his own despair, all England, from old maiden ladies who read and shrieked and read again, to the dandies and macaronis at the clubs, felt that the spirit of the hour had spoken and had uttered what every one was burning to listen to. Here, at last, was that passion the false semblance of which they had cheated themselves with in Monk Lewis and Kotzebue; passion as real and fierce as anything of which the Middle Ages could boast, yet mightily modern and with a distinguished pessimistic note that was new in this Western world. Open neckcloths became the only wear. People of fashion dared to look beyond the drawing-room and the coffee-house and the club and to realize that they were perhaps something more than exquisitely fashioned social automata. Byron gave aristocratic sanction to the rebel heart.

Intense, passionate personal experience of all kinds — this was Byron's ideal. The experience

was to be won for the most part through action;
Byron was not subtle and did not anticipate the
modern dilettante's refined methods of savouring
life at second hand and enriching one's spirit
imaginatively and by proxy. Life meant to him the
play of a fiercely egoistic will in the search for self-
realization. Through adventure, through travel,
through intrigue, through love, the craving of the
individual for overwhelmingly vivid emotion was
perpetually to be gratified. In eighteenth-century
literature, only emotions had been expressed and
sanctioned such as men could share in common, —
such as made for the safety of a conventionally
wrought social organism. In Byron the individual
came to his rights with a vengeance, and indeed
came to more than his rights. Byron once for all
opened a career for talent in the matter of emotion;
every man was to feel as richly and intensely as the
gods had given him power to feel. The needs of
his own heart, not the needs of the social organism,
were to be the test of the fitness of his feeling.
"Custom's scale" was false; and conventional
society was through and through made what it was
by misleading traditions and prescriptions. From
all these the individual should turn away and
should turn toward Nature. Individual passion
was working out for itself a new destiny; and conventional society had to come in for much random
abuse as well as for quite justifiable criticism and
invective.

What Wordsworth did for the spiritual regeneration of the century has become, of course, a very
familiar story. In point of fact, however, Wordsworth's influence made itself felt at the start with
surprising slowness. He had been publishing his
earliest poems while Byron was still trundling hoop
and quarrelling with his nurse, and the first edition
of the *Lyrical Ballads* had appeared when Byron
was only ten years old. Yet not till 1829 — so
Lord Houghton notes — did Wordsworth — five
years after Byron's death — begin to supplant the
poet of *Childe Harold* and the *Giaour* in the favour
of University youth. Wordsworth was essentially
the most conservative of the Romanticists; and for
that reason his vogue came more slowly, and for
that reason, too, his influence has been farther-
reaching and more permanent. Like all the
Romanticists Wordsworth was anti-conventional;
but, unlike so many of them, he was never for a
moment essentially anti-social.

Wordsworth's anti-conventionalism showed itself
in many ways and forms. He contemned "the
world" with a spiritual scorn that was in its own
fashion as withering as Byron's cynical satire in
Don Juan. His hatred of conventional life utters
itself alike in his poetry and in his correspondence.
In *Tintern Abbey* he bewails the unloveliness of
ordinary human intercourse and grieves over the
"rash judgments," "the sneers of selfish men," the
"greetings where no kindness is," which make up

so large a part of it. In one of his letters he describes the round of idleness and frivolity in which the frequenter of routs and assemblies spends his time, and asserts that the man who leads such an existence can have no insight into poetry. Wordsworth loathed the artificial life of the town and he never would have consented to accept, as M. Sully-Prudhomme in *La Justice* accepts, the modern city as being the treasure-house and the symbol of the best that the human race has wrought out for itself. At times, it almost seems as if Wordsworth would have liked to have all men and women take to the woods. Moreover, Wordsworth's romantic anti-conventionalism shows itself not only in his attacks on the world, but in the positive parts of his moral doctrine. He was bent on regenerating the individual human being, on transforming him in many ways, on waking in him manifold new instincts, new feelings, new passions, and new aspirations, on making him over almost as radically, so it sometimes seems, as even Byron wished.

Yet despite all his hatred of old artificial conventions and despite all his desire to bring new tracts of experience within reach of the individual, Wordsworth was not for a moment anti-social. In all his tinkering with the human type, he regarded the complex of moral affections that had been traditionally approved in English life as sacrosanct. The love of husband for wife, and of parents for

children, all the domestic sanctities, the veneration
of the Christian for the Church, and the allegiance
of the citizen to the state, and of the common man
to all the squirearchical powers above him — these
Wordsworth reverenced as the essential elements
of individual worth; he had no Shelleyan mission
to manufacture a totally new brand of human
nature, no cynical Byronic rage for destruction for
its own delightful sake.

Wherein then consisted Wordsworth's regenerating influence, — the indubitable renovation of the
spirit that his poetry wrought and was meant to
effect? This influence came in a twofold way.
The old affections and instincts received through
Wordsworth's imaginative treatment of them a
special new virtue; and they were also supplemented and reënforced by new masses of delicate
and tender and ennobling emotion that Wordsworth was the first to experience, to express with
imaginative power, and to infect others with.

Through his transcendentalism Wordsworth gave
a new meaning not simply to Physical Nature but
to Human Nature as well. Securely convinced as
he was of the existence of an Infinite Spiritual
Power that revealed itself in the conscience of man
and also ministered to him through the splendour
and beauty of Nature, — embracing the individual
on all sides with caressing and sustaining symbolism, — Wordsworth believed, further, that the
humblest of human creatures, by yielding himself

obediently to the influence of this Power and ful-
filling its mandates, could reach true dignity and
grandeur. Every one knows Wordsworth's trans-
figured Leech-gatherer. He and his transfiguration
are examples of the kind of redemption that
Wordsworth sought to work throughout the range
of common life. He aimed to simplify and inten-
sify life, — to emphasize the primal affections and
instincts and duties, to give them new grace and
glory by a spiritual sanction, and to confer on the
most ordinary offices of life a certain mystical
beauty through portraying them as watched by
Nature with a kind of conspiring approval.

But Wordsworth did not simply work transform-
ingly upon the primal elements of human nature;
he gave to his fellows what was almost a new spiritual sense; he waked in them a new, delicate
instinct for beauty; he stirred in them new forms
of imaginative sympathy. Often he gets the credit
of having invented Nature; and in very truth the
peculiar modern feeling that nature and man are
close of kin and speak a common tongue first comes
into English poetry through Wordsworth. His
transcendentalism changed nature into a living
spiritual presence, thrillingly responsive to man's
spiritual moods and needs. The brazen heavens
that had weighed over the eighteenth century
became "the soft blue sky" that "melts into the
heart." The "horrid rocks" that had daunted the
men of the eighteenth century, or that had at most

stirred them to rhetorical admiration as before
cleverly wrought stage-scenery, became the haunted
abode of "the sleep that is among the lonely hills."
Everywhere in nature Wordsworth found spirit
waiting for recognition — gracious meanings exquisitely involved in the meshes of beautiful
colours and sounds, in the flight of the lark, in
the dancing of daffodils, in the trumpets of the
cataract; man's own spirit, in sublimated form,
divinely smiling out from behind the apparently
fortuitous play of the atoms. Everywhere he discovered, as Shelley said of him half-mockingly, "a
soul in sense." And this fine spiritual irritability
in the presence of nature was a permanent gift of
his to the English temperament. Many later poets
have felt and interpreted the symbolic challenge
of nature more subtly, but none more nobly and
pervasively.

And so one might go through the other Romantic
poets and trace out by analysis the æsthetic and
ethical winnings they garnered, the new kinds of
spiritual experience and the new modes of bliss and
of woe that they explored and made possible. Keats
is perhaps the least easily brought under the
Romantic formula; yet indubitably he belongs
there, despite the common talk about his Hellenism. There was never a greater master of "natural
magic" than the poet of *La Belle Dame sans Merci*.
"A *wild* and harmonizèd tune" it was that his
"spirit," as he himself says of Endymion, "struck

from all the beautiful." The beauty that he
created is an iridescent beauty, pulsingly indis-
tinct in its outlines, shimmering with elusive suggestions, not the firm, plastic beauty of Pagan art.
In Keats the senses, so pitifully neglected by the
eighteenth century, which looked, as Dr. Johnson
said, "for large appearances" and rarely wrote
with the eye on the object, came once more into
luxurious possession of the world. If Wordsworth
found a soul in sense, Keats found senses in the
soul. More nearly, perhaps, than any other poet
except Dante Gabriel Rossetti he exorcised the
Demon of the Abstract from the world of poetry.
He could not even measure empty distance or blank
time without striking into life images of beauty.

Moreover, in Keats's poetry the division between
the Romantic world of dreams and the actual
world of everyday fact is marked even more
clearly than it is in other Romantic poetry of the
time. Wordsworth and Byron, for example, both
rebelled against the tyranny of the actual; but
their awareness of the life they protested against
shows itself through the intensity or the fierceness
of their criticisms upon it. Keats for the most
part serenely disregards conventional life and all
its concerns and customs. There are, to be sure, in
Endymion two passages where he fantastically
breaks into outspoken scorn of the base interests
and false standards that rule in the practical world.
At the opening of Book iii., he describes the gro-

Bronze clarions awake and faintly bruit,
Where long ago a giant battle was ;
And from the turf a lullaby doth pass
In every place where infant Orpheus slept.''

War and political intrigue and all that has hap-
pened or happens on the crust of the earth become
at last the stuff that dreams are made of, — serve
simply to wake new vibrations in the beauty-lover's
temperament. The two sorts of bliss, to be sure,
that Keats most exalts are feelings that link the
individual to others; among passionate moods,
those that have "the chief intensity" are "friendship and love." Yet even these passionate moods
as Keats represents them really have their rewards
in themselves; they are moods of "ardent listless-
ness" that have no issue in the world of conventional routine. Keats's heroes never do aught save
wander ecstatically over the surface of the earth
and through the depths of the sea, or make love in
a lady's chamber. Even Hyperion's most superlative act is a magnificently picturesque entrance
into his palace. One has but to compare Keats's
heroes with Landor's—Endymion with Gebir—and
Keats's moods with Landor's to see how subjective
Keats is, how the world becomes for him merely a
great forcing-house for passion and rich entangle-
ments of feeling, how entirely his earth and his
moods and his aspirations are different from those
that enter into the conventional drama of practical
life, and how little they can receive the sanction

c

of the *common* sense.   Through all these qualities
of his genius, through his remoteness from ordinary life and his exquisite eccentricity, Keats
reveals himself as essentially Romantic.

When we turn from poetry to prose we find that
the formula that has been suggested as summing
up the Romantic movement still holds true.   In
its most characteristic forms the prose, like the
poetry of this period is used for the enrichment of
the inner life of the individual rather than for the
closer knitting of the bonds that bind men together
in conventional life.   Prose like poetry works for
the spiritualization of humanity rather than for its
organization.   In the pursuit of this somewhat un-
prosaic end, prose takes on many of the characteristics of poetry and strives in manifold ways to win
new expressiveness.   It gives over its monopolizing interest in abstract ideas and generalizations,
becomes aware of the surface of life, and tries to
portray the splendour and the magnificence of the
outside world as this world beats against thrilling
senses.   It gains often an intensely personal note,
and a tone and a rhythm that are almost lyrical.
Its surface glows with a figurative richness and
with a warmth and a colour that to Swift or to
Dr. Johnson would have seemed indecorous and
even grotesque.   The Preface of the *Lyrical Ballads,* as has already been noted, claimed for the
poetic interpretation of life superiority over the
prose interpretation.   This claim, the great prose-

writers of the period implicitly or explicitly granted. And they therefore were more or less consciously drawn to bring prose, their own mode of expression, as close as they might to the idiom of the gods. De Quincey's so-called "impassioned prose" works out and expresses Romantic ideals with an art that is deliberate and elaborate. Lamb, Hazlitt, and Leigh Hunt all accomplish, in one way or another, that peculiar redemption of the commonplace, in terms of intense personal feeling, in which the essence of Romantic art consists.

Characteristic of all these artists is the return for models of excellence to writers earlier than the age of Queen Anne, often to writers of the Elizabethan period. De Quincey's sarcastic strictures on the incompetent literalness of Swift's prose style have become traditional instances of Romantic prejudice; the savage Dean is challenged to write a description of the pageantry of Belshazzar's feast, and because of his alleged prosy inability, he is scorned as a mere base servitor in the train of art. Coleridge's devotion to Jeremy Taylor and to the splendid eloquence of even earlier divines passed into a byword. Lamb's first important literary venture was *John Woodvil*, a tragedy in the Elizabethan manner; and his *Specimens of English Dramatic Poets* (1808) contained delicately impressionistic criticism of the passion and power of the Elizabethan drama — criticism that sent readers by scores to the long-neglected works of Marlowe, Webster, and Ford.

The fantastically archaic beauty of Lamb's own
prose style would show how deeply he had been
subdued to the spell of sixteenth- and seventeenth-
century prose, even were his essays not so continually outspoken as they are in their devotion to
Isaak Walton, to Fuller, and to Burton.

Nor is the substance that enters into the prose of
Lamb, De Quincey, and Hazlitt less Romantic in
quality than their style.   Lamb's whim converts
the commonest object it plays over into something
new and delicately individual, fashioned cunningly
out of Lamb's moods and fancies and imaginative
associations.   Was there ever a quainter change
than that which the London chimney-sweep goes
through in the pages of Lamb's essay?   He comes
out all cobwebbed over with gossamer beauty, —
a sort of Prince from the Land of Droll Dreaming,
a sublimated little symbol of thoughts and feelings that in actual life are leagues out of his ken.
To assure one's self of the Romantic note in Lamb,
one need but compare an essay of this sort with
Addison's or Steele's essays.   Lamb is subjective, moody, imaginative, fantastic, always tremulously aware of the mystery that lurks behind
the commonplace, though rarely expressing this
directly.

Nor, indeed, is Hazlitt's Romanticism any less
unmistakable.   His essays are full of querulous
protest against the checks and scorns to which
conventional life subjects the special soul; full

of pathetic appeals to Nature for redress, and of
Rousseau-like passionate portrayal of natural
scenery; often poignant in their utterance of personal sorrow and grieving; often lyrical in their
tone and movement; at times, audacious in their
imagery.

As for De Quincey, almost the whole range of
Romantic effect is to be found in his impassioned
prose; he is the greatest and the most representative of Romantic prose-artists. More pertina-
ciously than any other prose-writer he tries to carry
prose beyond its old-time boundaries and to give it
a new emotional and imaginative scope. Perhaps
the most persistent mannerism to be traced in his
methods of communicating impressions of beauty
and power is his frequent recourse to a kind of visionary second-sight. Doubtless this trick of mind
and of treatment was fostered, if nothing more, by
his opium-eating. The beauty of the trance, the
splendour of the vision, the mystery of the seventh
heaven and of Plato's sphere lie over the most
characteristic scenes of his prose. The chambers
of the air suddenly open, and on some insignifi-
cant portion of common life there rains down influence through infinite distances from a mysterious
spiritual world, which thus reveals itself as embracing common life, pressing upon it as it were
on all sides, though from measureless distances,
terribly involving it in momentous issues for good
or evil. The mysteries that infinite space may

hold in concealment, the mysteries that may have been enacted in past æons of time, or that still may be waiting in endless perspective — these De Quincey suggests with necromantic power, so that before them the imagination is appalled. Moreover, he is often not content with suggesting these mysteries vaguely or symbolically; he actually opens before his readers, through the use of elaborately picturesque imagery, endless vistas to the outermost walls of space; or he dizzies the mind with ingenious mimicry of the never-ending flight of hours and days and years and centuries. Even in dealing with historical subjects, De Quincey, if he is bent on artistic effect, is apt to use, in working out his material, many of these same methods, so as to produce a visionary representation of life that carries with it an atmosphere of mystery and that at the same time has sensuous splendour. His *Flight of a Tartar Tribe* is the *Rime of the Ancient Mariner* done into prose, with a whole people's wanderings for the *motif* instead of one poor seaman's misadventure; De Quincey's prose almost rivals Coleridge's verse in giving to a tale the strenuous movement, the sustained sensuousness, as well as the mysteriousness, of a dream. Whatever enters into De Quincey's mind, — whether it be Oxford Street, or a wandering Malay, or poor Ann, the London waif, or Joan of Arc, — is transformed when it appears in his impassioned prose, in this same marvellous fashion, rendered exceeding mystical, shimmeringly beautiful, and irresistibly credible withal, as if it had indeed been spun into opium-visions by the "just, subtle, and mighty" spirit whose home was in the famous "little golden receptacle." One is sometimes tempted to make this spirit and this receptacle the symbol and the talisman of the whole Romantic movement.

The preceding analyses of poets and prose-writers will perhaps have justified in some measure the formulas which have been suggested as summing up the most characteristic literature of the first quarter of our century. In England there was never a Romantic school as there was in both Germany and France. The English poems and prose-writings which have just been analyzed were in many and important particulars radically and almost irreconcilably unlike. Their authors were never in league in the pursuit of a common and clearly recognized end, artistic or moral; indeed, they were often not personally known to each other, or they were even outspoken foes. Yet, as it were in spite of themselves, they gave to their poems and their prose certain common characteristics; their imaginations, through a sort of secret understanding, acknowledged a kinship, which the men themselves would have been the last to claim. So, for example, there is a curious likeness to be traced in the heroes of the great poems of this period. These heroes — whether Greek Endymions, mock-mediæval Childe Harolds, Cumberland Pedlars, or

worshippers of Alastor — are all lonely, dreamy
wanderers. They are adventurers in the world of
the spirit, searchers after new sensations, new
moods, new strains of passion, "ideal-blind" en-
thusiasts of one sort or another. They are questers
after the Holy Grail, followers of the vision,
aspirers after some new form of the blessèd life.
They all trust the imagination and the heart and
have scant respect for the understanding and the
reason.   And this striking similarity of theirs
comes from the fact that, diverse as they are in
equipment and in fortune, they are one and all
essentially personifications of the spirit of a Romantic age, and symbolize in their ambitions its one
preoccupation. The Romantic imagination, through
its inevitable bias toward the creation of these
dreamy wanderers, reveals the essential striving of
the Romantic movement.

The age was an age of expansion. The human
spirit was reaching out delicately or strenuously in
many ways for new forms of experience. It was
emancipating itself once and for all from the hard
and fast restrictions of prosaic eighteenth-century
life. It sought out and conned the story of its own
past, and found there a *naïve* passionateness and
a decorative splendour which rationalism and
"refinement" had later drained from both national
and individual life, and which the new age was
longing to realize once more in its own experience.
The heart, the senses, and the imagination reas-

serted their rights after the long tyranny of the
understanding. The senses became alert and
thrillingly sensitive; they learned to catch all the
pretty configuration and the shadow-play of the
surface of the earth; and they gathered, too,
the impressions of awful beauty and power in
nature to which the eighteenth century had been
blind. Moreover, beneath what the tremulous
senses discerned in nature, the quickened spirit
divined everywhere a subtle play of energy cor-
respondent to its own, and it dreamed the dream of
transcendentalism and found the universe instinct
with symbolism and spiritual meanings. In short,
the whole nature of man was once more vitalized
into free, confident play after the long period of
paralyzing over-intellectualism which had so curiously prevailed since the days of Descartes and
Hobbes. And as the result of this mysticism and
passion and audacious dreaming, the human spirit
won many new aptitudes and new powers and
acquired a new range of sensitiveness to a myriad
hitherto unperceived shades of beauty and feeling.

But all this was accomplished at the risk or the
expense of conventional society. These dreamers,
both the poets themselves and their heroes, were
scorners of commonplace life, and cultivated their
souls at the expense of their citizenship. Not one
of Byron's or Shelley's or Keats's heroes can
be pictured going intelligently and successfully
through the ordinary round of a sane man's duties.

A state whose citizens should frame themselves on the model of Childe Harold or Laon or even of Wordsworth's Pedlar would soon be brought into a very sadly disorganized plight. Moreover, the unregulated wills, the morbid nerves, and the erratic lives of the poets themselves, — these, too, seemed almost to offer palpable proof of the absurdity of the ideals that the poets embodied in their verse. And so it was that in the characteristic literature of the period that followed the age of Romanticism, remote and untempered Romantic dreaming was indulged in with less and less confidence — sometimes, perhaps, with self-conscious sadness, or with self-pitying scorn, or with despairing regret, but hardly at all with the old-time fervent faith; and men turned back to conventional life with a sense that it must after some fashion be reckoned with more seriously than the Idealists and the Romanticists had been apt to think.

THE RETURN TO CONVENTIONAL LIFE

By 1824 the Romantic impulse, pure and simple, had in poetry very nearly spent its creative force. Keats and Shelley were dead. Scott was long since given over to prose. Coleridge was spinning metaphysical webs in the fastnesses of Highgate. Even Wordsworth, who lived half through the century, published after 1824 only a single volume of verse that had not been written long before that date. In 1824, too, Byron died and Carlyle, the great prose-foe of Byronic *Welt-Schmerz*, published his first volume — significantly enough a translation of Goethe's *Wilhelm Meister*. The wayward dreaming of Romanticism had had its day, and in the characteristic poetry of the following period a new relation to the conventional world of everyday fact showed itself continually.

Great as were the gains that accrued to the human spirit from the Romanticists' passionate questing after new experience of all sorts, the limitations of the Romantic genius, and its dangerous eccentricities became clearer and clearer as this genius worked itself out into thorough expression. The Romanticists were web-spinners and

fancy-mongers, who were apt to move through life
in a kind of divine bewilderment. They were
beauty-blind and music-deaf. They lived inside
their own individual heads, in the circle of their
own eccentric personalities, — in fantastic air-spun
worlds of their own devising. They had little wish
or power to grapple with commonplace facts either
in life or in art. The world portrayed in their
poetry is a visionary world quite out of the ken
of ordinary folk, surcharged with strangeness, and
treacherous to the uninitiated. Their favourite
characters are uncanny creatures, spectral, prone to
posing, psychologically shallow. Fancy Dr. Samuel
Johnson's growls of disapproval at the Wanderer
in Shelley's *Alastor*, who goes soliloquizing through
impossible landscapes on a hopeless quest for impossible beauty, and dies in despair to the light of
an impossible moon. Thomas Love Peacock has
put into a cleverly satirical summary the essential
absurdity that seems to the worldly-wise man to
lurk in Byron's romantic despair: "You talk,"
says Mr. Hilary to Mr. Cypress, "like a Rosi-
crucian who will love nothing but a sylph, who
does not believe in the existence of a sylph, and
who yet quarrels with the whole universe for not
containing a sylph." The wordly-wise man does
not stake his happiness on the problematical
favours of an ideal that would not exist unless
he himself took the trouble to call it into being.
Romantic dreamers were victims of their own mag-

gots, so it seemed to the common-sense onlooker;
and incontestably their overmuch indulgence in
dreaming tended to destroy in them the controlling
sense of their kinship with ordinary men. All of
them, save perhaps Scott, made war, though with
varying degrees of bitterness, on custom and convention. They were creatures of whim and caprice.
They shunned the routine of ordinary life. They
sought to wrest for themselves from the world, each
in his own way, some individual bliss. Even the
moral Wordsworth went "booing" his verses over
the Westmoreland hills in a fashion that would
have made Jeffrey gasp and stare. Their heroes,
from Byron's and Shelley's adventurers to Wordsworth's Peter Bell and Idiot Boy, were at odds with
society. Consciously or unconsciously the Romanticists were preaching the gospel of fad and of eccentricity. They were underrating the worth of
tradition and precedent and the established order.
They were audaciously challenging reason and common sense, and were letting impulse and unauthen-
ticated instinct run riot. In their fostering of
spirit they became sadly contemptuous of the intricate relationships — prejudices, beliefs, customs,
fashions, laws — that unite actual living men and
women into a complex, prosperously working social
organism. Romantic poets had a genius for *tran-
scending* everyday concerns and the facts and per-
sonages of the work-day world. God, Freedom,
Immortality, Nature — these were the presences

and the themes that fixed their gaze and domi-
nated their imaginations. Their own souls, their
own moods, their exaltations and despairs, their
aspirations toward the infinite, their languors or
ecstasies on the moors or beside the sea-breakers
or under the free cope of heaven, — these were
their preoccupations, not the turmoil of the town
or the complexities of actual human character.
Their poetry was the expression of brooding loneliness and concerned their own relations to God
and to Nature, not their relations to other men.
As a consequence of all this it followed that Romanticism bid fair to lead to social disintegration;
or at any rate, it encouraged and fostered a wide
variety of dangerously morbid individualities hard
to be reconciled and welded together into a well-
wrought social fabric. Because of its subjectivity,
its whimsical emotionalism, its wayward imaginativeness, Romanticism tended, while developing
the individual spirit into rich variety of life, to
shatter conventional society, and to replace its
compact organization of harmonious types with a
loosely related mass of abnormal personalities.
One cannot but sympathize with Matthew Arnold's
impatient outcry over Shelley's droll domesticity.
Brook Farm in America was for a time very ap-
petizing make-believe, but it had not within its
organization the blood and the sinew of reality
necessary to insure permanence and complexity
of life.

Such were in' general the dangerous tendencies
that after 1824 were more and more clearly discerned in Romanticism; and it was because of this
discernment that the characteristic poetry of the
following period took a new tone and a new direc-
tion. Not, however, that the poetry of the later
period repudiated Romance; not that it returned
to the arid intellectual habit of eighteenth-century
life. What it really aimed to do was to avoid the
extravagance of the Romanticists and to realize
more intimately and successfully what was vital
and quintessential in Idealism. The new poets
took into their blood and tempers the Romantic
increment; they taught their hearts to beat to the
tunes of Romantic rhythms; their senses were
trained to all the delicacy and alertness that Romantic experience made possible; their imaginations ran to and fro through nature with much of
the fine Romantic instinct for hidden symbolism.
They dreamed the dreams of the Romanticists, and
yielded themselves with one and another Romantic
seer to the Vision on the Mount. But they could
not be content with the evasive visionariness of
Romanticism or with its remoteness from actual
life. They felt more and more keenly the claims
of the commonplace and the conventional. They
saw the evil trick of Romance — its way of dispers-
ing itself in iridescent mists and leaving the crass
world of fact still unlovely and sordid. And so
they came to feel the need of bringing down the

Vision on the Mount, the Idealists' dream of beauty, into the rumouring, turbulent life below, and of converting Romance into a vital transforming force that should actually recreate in terms of beauty that common life, a loyal sharing in which can alone enable the individual, be he dreamer or worker, to fulfil the whole scope of his nature and reach his utmost effectiveness. A persistent striving to secure a synthesis between the Ideal and the Actual is characteristic of the poetry of the post-Romantic period.

This period extends roughly to 1860, and includes the most important poems of Arthur Hugh Clough, Elizabeth Barrett Browning, and Matthew Arnold; its typical representative in prose is Thomas Carlyle. Much of the work of Tennyson and Browning was also given to the world before 1860; but these poets passed beyond the post-Romantic period both in the years of their activity and in the spirit in which they interpreted life; and they can therefore be better considered by themselves.

Arthur Hugh Clough cannot be ranked, on the basis of pure poetic achievement, in the same class with Arnold and Mrs. Browning. He has left, to be sure, in the *Bothie of Tober na Vuolich*, a richly fragrant idyll of country life, which is almost unique in its union of humour and transfiguring passion in the treatment of everyday English incident. A few of his lyrics, too, where fate seems to have guided him into melody, are memorable for their simple beauty of phrase as well as for their spiritual ardour.   But in the main — let it be said with all possible respect to his eulogist in *Thyrsis* — Clough was but a bungling workman in verse.   He must nearly always be read with allowances.   And yet his poetry is historically of high interest because of its sensitive reflection of the spirit of his age.   His *Dipsychus* is a delicately sure, analytic record, half-lyrical and half-dramatic, of the typical moods of sad recollection, distrust, hesitation, and final acquiescence, with which many men of his day, who had listened long to the music of romantic poetry, turned back at last from vague dreaming and laid hold of the tasks of conventional life.

The scene of the poem is laid in Venice, and at the start the hero, Dipsychus, the Double-minded, a young Englishman, of exceptional fineness of temperament, comes before us very much in the guise of one of the Romantic Wanderers of the preceding poetic age.   He soliloquizes over the fantastic splendour of the scenes around him, bewails in good set terms the vileness of human society, and turns with true Romantic queasiness to nature for consolation : —

> " Clear stars above, thou roseate westward sky,
>   Take up my being into yours ; assume
>   My sense to know you only ; steep my brain
>   In your essential purity."

D

Significantly, however, this early passage is the only one in the poem where Nature is apostrophized or where the suffering special soul turns to her for refuge from actual life. Moreover, in Clough's poem, the reader feels from the very start that he is looking out upon actual throngs of moving men and women, is caught in the veritable swirl of the world's business, and is not, as he always is in reading the Romantic poets, wandering in some excellent remote region filled with dream-splendours and a fantastic populace.

As the poem goes on, Dipsychus scans the drama of conventional life, feels the charm of its whim and vigour and brilliance, is stirred with a sense of its energy and stupendous, unquestioning onrush after tangible good; and yet he revolts from its selfishness, its carnal preoccupations, its pitiful narrowness of interest, and its inveterate frivolity. He glides in a gondola through all the gnarring turmoil as one might let one's self be swept by a dream safely through uncanny noises and threatening complications; he lulls himself with fancies of what the world ought to be and with the images of beauty and truth that his heart summons before him. And as he feeds his desire on these golden imaginations, the refrain sounds again and again in an undertone, —

"Life should be as the gondola."

At last, however, when he sets foot on shore, he sadly concedes that "Life is not as the gondola;"

and he passes into a new mood. Life is not dreaming, it is action; "live we must;" and he turns to the Spirit of this World who has been all the time beside him, carping Mephistopheles-wise at what he deems Dipsychus's sentimental maunderings, and demands how he is to become practical and mingle successfully in the great game of life.

The Spirit in answer welcomes with fine satirical humour the prodigal who seems repenting of his idealism. He ridicules Dipsychus's late dreams as "but moonshine after all," "airy blisses, skiey joys, of vague romantic girls and boys." He reproaches him with having made "mows to the blank sky" quite long enough. He sneers at Dipsychus's silly slavery to deluding visions; Dipsychus, he declares, has been walking about with his eyes shut, —

> "Treating for facts the self-made hues that flash
> On tight-pressed pupils."

And finally he chants a prettily satirical lyric in praise of submission to the God of this World : —

> "Submit, submit !
> For tell me then, in earth's great laws
> Have you found any saving clause,
> Exemption special granted you
> From doing what the rest must do ?
> Of common sense who made you quit
> And told you you'd no need of it,
> Nor to submit ?

> "To move on angel's wings were sweet ;
> But who would therefore scorn his feet ?

It cannot walk up to the sky;
It therefore will lie down and die.
Rich meats it don't obtain at call;
It therefore will not eat at all.
Poor babe, and yet a babe of wit!
But common-sense, not much of it,
Or 'twould submit,
Submit, submit!"

After a good deal of crackling badinage of this
sort, the Spirit finally grows more serious, promises
to teach Dipsychus "the Second Reverence — for
things around," — the allusion to Goethe is worth
noting, — and sets forth the absolute need there is
for the individual to accept the bonds of customary life with all their chafing limitations, if he is
not to be a mere helpless, fantastic, isolated unit.

"This stern necessity of things
On every side our being rings;
Our sallying eager actions fall
Vainly against that iron wall.
Where once her finger points the way,
The wise thinks only to obey;
Take life as she has ordered it,
And come what may of it, submit,
Submit, submit."

During all the Spirit's raillery and haranguing,
Dipsychus has been considering and reconsider-
ing his relation to the world. He has felt the
cogency of the Spirit's words; he has realized his
own remoteness from fact, his impotence, his idle
dreaminess. Yet he has shrunk from the sordid-
ness of common life; he has rebelled against the

need of losing his personal stamp and becoming a
mere unrecognizable portion of the world's mechanical routine; he has inveighed against the triviality
and commonness of the tasks at which the individual must set himself, and against the lack of all
chance for original and noble effort; and he has
bewailed the apparent aimlessness of the stupid
world-process to which he must enslave himself.
Nevertheless he finally makes his choice and com-
mits himself to the region of fact.

Yet after all it is not to the power of the half-
malevolent Spirit of this World that Dipsychus
resigns his will; and just here lies the crucial
difference by virtue of which the conventionality of
the new age was to be something far nobler than
the conventionality of the eighteenth century.
Although Dipsychus finally elects for the world
of action and resigns himself to practical life, he
nevertheless remains in his heart true to his idealistic dreaming.   He declares himself, perhaps a bit
grotesquely, "a kidnapped child of heaven"; and
it is with the memory of his celestial origin still
alive and active within him that he surrenders himself to temporary thraldom.   So he exclaims to the
Spirit of this World : —

> "Not for thy service, thou imperious fiend,
> Not to do thy work, or the like of thine ;
> Not to please thee, O base and fallen spirit !
> But One Most High, Most True, whom without thee
> It seems I cannot serve.   O the misery
> That one must truck and practise with the world

To gain the vantage-ground to assail it from ;
To set upon the Giant one must first,
O Perfidy ! have eat the Giant's bread.
If I submit, it is but to gain time
And arms and stature."

And so the Dreamer enters the field of action with
the resolve to utilize loyally the delicacy, the sensitiveness, the spiritual alertness that the Romanticists have developed in him, to embody in the
harsh material of conventional fact the dreams he
has long nourished, and to realize in the regions of
common endeavour the Vision on the Mount.

In Mrs. Browning's poetry there is both more and
less Romanticism than in Clough's.   In many ways
she seemed doomed in the very nature of things to
be a mere dreamer; as a woman, with a woman's
tremulous nerve-fibres and delicate sensibility, as a
woman of genius, and, therefore, exceptionally im-
pressionable and imaginative, and, above all as an
invalid, shut for many years within the hothouse
precincts of a sick-chamber, she seemed consigned
beyond redress to a life of subjective moodiness
and of visionary remoteness from fact.   Yet in
truth in reading her poetry we are taken far more
into the thick of the tumult of living, into the
murk and the flaring confusion, and among the
blows and the counter-blows of the actual battle of
life than we are in reading Keats or Shelley, or indeed any of the Romanticists.   She belonged vitally
to her age.   Even in her solitude she had felt the

stream of tendency that was setting back toward conventional life. Her longer poems, *Casa Guidi Windows*, *Lady Geraldine's Courtship*, *Aurora Leigh*, all strive to catch the very lineaments of the human drama that was around her as she wrote.

And indeed that Art should thus deal courageously with the immediate facts of daily life was a cardinal tenet of Mrs. Browning's. She has expounded her Theory of Art elaborately in various parts of *Aurora Leigh*, — a theory too involved and abstract to be summarized here. An essential part of the theory, however, is her conception of the poet's task and of his relations to his fellows. The poet is not to be a weaver of visions, a spinner of decorative beauty, or a lonely specialist in eccentric moods; he is to be "God's truth-teller," the authentic interpreter of the innermost meaning of daily events, the revealer of the core of spiritual energy that utters itself sensuously in the often apparently haphazard fact and incident of the cosmic-process. He is not to run like a recreant to the past in search of his subjects: "I do distrust," Mrs. Browning declares,

> "the poet who discerns
> No character or glory in his times,
> And trundles back his soul five hundred years,
> Past moat and drawbridge, into a castle-court."

He is to preserve in his verse the living image of his own day and generation: —

> " Never flinch,
> But still unscrupulously epic, catch
> Upon the burning lava of a song
> The full-veined, heaving, double-breasted age."

He should be able to find even in the most sordid aspects of life, and in the most seemingly vulgar characters, meaning and suggestiveness that shall redeem them and give them imaginative power: —

> " Humanity is great ;
> And if I would not rather pore upon
> An ounce of common, ugly human dust,
> An artisan's palm or a peasant's brow,
> Unsmooth, ignoble, save to me and God,
> Than track old Nilus to his silver roots,
> And wait on all the changes of the moon
> Among the mountain peaks of Tuscany,
> (Until her magic crystal round itself
> For many a witch to see in) — set it down
> As weakness, — strength by no means."

Mrs. Browning's longest narrative poem, *Aurora Leigh,* is conceived and wrought out in close harmony with these ideals of what should be the sphere and the aim of poetry. The story concerns the life of a young girl, half-Italian and half-English, who grows up in an old-fashioned country house in England in the midst of books and of nature, who chooses letters for a profession, and who goes to London and captures the world with her poetry. Her love for her cousin — a keenly intellectual social reformer, an apostle of statistics and political economy — furnishes the conventional *motif* of passion for the narrative. But though thus ostensibly portraying the life of a visionary girl and though continually revealing the world through her eyes, the poem is really an interpretation and criticism of the entire age in which it was written. The characters are drawn from the whole range of English society; the incident is widely varied and typical, and yet not extravagant or out of the bounds of daily experience; the analysis of motive, and of the play of the social forces which in large measure determine the action, is searching and suggestive; and the poem is continually — too continually for the taste of some uncourageous readers — unfolding the ways of God to man as they reveal themselves through the fortunes and the fates of the actors in the story. There is withal much glowing rhetoric — often brilliantly imaginative, albeit sometimes florid and hysterical — concerning the economic and social and artistic questions that were most canvassed in the later fifties. And everywhere the reader is kept within sound of the busy rumour of daily life: he breathes the actual air of the smoky London streets; he explores squalid tenements; he watches the pageantry of church weddings; he flashes on railway journeys across the continent; he is never for long allowed to lose sight of the expressive visage of the great world of fact.

As a result of her absorbing interest in the human drama, nature plays no such rôle in Mrs. Browning's

poetry as with the Romanticists. Nature she knows
with an intimate command of detail that is surprising when one thinks of her long years of illness.
But she never or rarely makes a deliberate emotional study of nature for its own sake or gives
herself over to lonely dreaming in the midst of
nature. She offers her readers no lyric of the West
Wind or of the Skylark or of Mont Blanc, and no
"Tintern Abbey." She sees nature a trifle askance;
she cannot for long in her narrative poems desert
her men and women; and even in her shorter poems,
it is with the human heart — not perhaps her own
— that her imagination busies itself rather than
with nature. Nature is secondary with her. True,
some of her passing sketches of landscapes are
surprisingly broad and vigorous — as, for example,
that of the Alps from the train on the way to Italy.
Moreover, in one other kind of sketching from the
outside world, Mrs. Browning attains almost unique
brilliance and truth of effect, namely, in her swift
impressions of great cities: —

> "So, I mused
> Up and down, up and down, the terraced streets,
> The glittering Boulevards, the white colonnades
> Of fair fantastic Paris who wears trees
> Like plumes, as if man made them; spire and tower
> As if they had grown by nature, tossing up
> Her fountains in the sunshine of the squares."

The beauty of Paris, a beauty that seems all spun
of gossamer and silver, and the spacious, airy ways

of the city, could hardly be more delicately and
surely captured and suggested.   There are parallel
studies of London — smudgy, and done in India ink
— which give the very texture of London air and
the slant of London roofs and chimney-pots.   Florence, too, Mrs. Browning puts impressionistically
before us with the same dexterous touch, — Florence
gleaming in Italian sunshine and with proper atmospheric modulations.   But all these sketches are, of
course, not of nature pure and simple, but of man's
handiwork in the outside world; so that here again
Mrs. Browning diverges from Romantic paths; she
turns from nature back toward man.

Yet, be it always remembered, she brings back
with her to real life, as Clough and his hero brought,
though even more valorously, faith in the ideal;
and she interprets both nature and man with a
sensitiveness and an insight that the Romanticists
had alone made possible.   Her whole theory of art
and of life involved a far-reaching and uncompro-
mising idealism.   There is a long passage in the
seventh book of *Aurora Leigh* that gives to this
idealism brilliantly imaginative and yet fairly formal expression, and brings it into close connection
with those conceptions of the poet and the artist as
revealers of hidden truth that have already been
noted.

> " A twofold world
> Must go to a perfect cosmos.   Natural things
> And spiritual, — who separates those two

In art, in morals, or the social drift,
Tears up the bond of Nature and brings death,
Paints futile pictures, writes unreal verse,
Leads vulgar days, deals ignorantly with men,
Is wrong in short at all points.

*   *   *   *   *   *

" Without the spiritual, observe,
The natural 's impossible ; no form,
No motion ! Without sensuous, spiritual
Is inappreciable ; — no beauty or power:
And in this twofold sphere the twofold man
(And still the artist is intensely a man)
Holds firmly by the natural, to reach
The spiritual beyond it, — fixes still
The type with mortal vision, to pierce through,
With eyes immortal, to the antetype
Some call the ideal."

In accordance with this doctrine, Mrs. Browning,
in her portrayal of conventional life, tries to exhibit
the forces that in the midst of the most prosaic
conditions are at work for the realization of ideal
ends ; she aims to confer dignity and splendour upon
human existence by showing that even in its worst
complications of sorrow and evil there are beauty
and good in the making.   And thus she endeavours
to bring about that synthesis between the Ideal
and the Actual of which the post-Romanticists so
keenly felt the need.

In the preface to one of his volumes of verse,
Matthew Arnold definitely condemned the personal
point of view of the Romanticists as unfitted for
the creation of poetry of the highest order.   The

poet, he urged, should be objective; he should emu-
late pagan art in its temperateness of mood, its
fine severity, and its burnished beauty.   But when
Arnold came to put his doctrine to the test, he
found that the spirit of the age was not to be thus
easily defied; that its vital impulse was not to be
held in check simply at the dictates of an academic
ideal.   Arnold had "learnt the lore" of the Romanticists "too well," and he could not keep out of
his verse the recollected airs of Romantic art.   His
Sohrab and Rustum and *Balder Dead*, written in
loyal illustration of his theory, are at best fairly
proficient academic exercises — too late to take the
Newdigate prize.   The poems by virtue of which
he lives are for the most part those in which
his personal moods utter themselves sincerely —
moods of tender grieving for the recollected glory
of the Romantic age.   M. Zola has described some
living French poet as having been touched by the
chilling finger of science.   The phrase fits Arnold
well.   He had been in his youth, as he himself
records in more than one poem, fervently enam-
oured of Romantic ideals; but he had later lost
the power of yielding himself to them uncritically
and sincerely.   His most characteristic note is an
elegiac note of regret for the waning of the glories
of the earlier age when faith was still on the earth.
He is the poet of a lost cause — the lost cause of
Romance.

Arnold's treatment of what may be called the

Wanderer-*motif* makes clear the change of mood
that parts him from the Romanticists. The traditional Wanderer of the Romantic poets is wholly
the victim of his own joy or teen; he follows
through regions of fantastic beauty after some elusive ideal of passionate bliss; he believes in himself utterly, whether he be Byron's Childe Harold
or one of Shelley's wan poets; and his creators too
— they believe in him implicitly and recount with
poignant sincerity his spiritual joys and woes. He
is indeed the imaginative embodiment of their
most vital impulse — their vagrant, unresting pursuit of new modes of bliss and pain, of new forms
of spiritual experience. Arnold's imagination has
also busied itself more than once with the fate of
a Wanderer — notably in the *Scholar-Gypsy* and in
Thyrsis. The Scholar-Gypsy, as one first encounters him, seems to have much of the old-time
Romantic turn of figure and cast of countenance;
every one remembers his "dark, vague eyes and
soft, abstracted air"; and every one remembers,
too, how he is represented in *Thyrsis* as seeking,
apparently in true Romantic wise, "a fugitive and
gracious light . . . shy to illumine"; he "wends
unfollowed"; he "must house alone"; onward
"he fares by his own heart inspired." Yet in
spite of the seeming resemblance of Arnold's Wanderers to the Romantic type, a little analysis will
show that the play of the poet's imagination as it
creates these later Wanderers is very different from

that which wrought out the Wanderers of an earlier age; and that the world through which these later Wanderers dream their way has also changed in significant wise.   Arnold's poems about Wanderers are all confessedly tender make-believe — exquisitely refined elaborations of an artistic theme; the Scholar-Gypsy is merely a legendary figure which Arnold's imagination captures from the pages of Glanvil and shapes with sad and gracious art into a symbol of Idealism.   Throughout the poem, while this charming visionary Wanderer is "waiting for the spark from heaven," he is followed by regretful and — shall we say? — half-patronizing,   worldly - wise   onlookers, — "light half-believers of our casual creeds," — whose "vague resolves" and speculative disillusionment set the standard of fact and convert the Scholar-Gypsy into a mere pathetic, though lovely, wraith. He is a phantom, for whose apparition the poet, tenderly as he treats him, half apologizes.   And the landscapes that he wanders through — these, too, are very different from purely Romantic landscapes, from the landscapes, for example, in *Alastor*.   They have none of the courageous and persuasive falseness of Shelley's landscapes.   Over them there broods "the soft canopy of English air"; they are wrought out with loving fidelity of detail; their "scarlet poppies," their "wide fields of breezy grass," their "green-muffled Cumner hills," and the rural figures, too, that move in the

midst of familiar scenes through homely rustic
tasks, all have the colour and accent of actual English life. *They* are incontestably real, and their
delicate truth and good faith but make the flitting
figure of the Scholar-Gypsy seem the more elusive,
and render him the more unmistakably a symbol,
imaginatively wrought out with conscious artistry.
For Arnold, Idealism has become but an undetain-
able reminiscence; the world of exquisite natural
fact defeats, even against the poet's wish, the spirit
of Romance.

This same tenderly heroic loyalty to ideals that
are still felt to be half-futile is expressed in the
famous *Stanzas from the Grande Chartreuse*. A
very well-known passage in the poem sets definitely
over against each other the earlier world of the
idealists and the modern world of conventional
experience — the flaunting world of science and
triumphant fact. Arnold elects for the world of
dreamers; his heart is with the "shy recluses,"
inheritors of the spirit of a visionary age, who
cannot reconcile themselves to the bewildering,
albeit splendid, pageantry of actual life. The passage is almost too trite to quote; but its extreme
appositeness will justify it.

> "Wandering between two worlds, one dead,
>   The other powerless to be born,
>   With nowhere yet to rest my head,
>   Like these, on earth I wait forlorn.
>   Their faith, my tears, the world deride —
>   I come to shed them at their side."

There follows in the poem a brilliantly picturesque passage describing the joy and the splendour of worldly life: troops flash by in the sun with pennons and plumes and lances; hunters gather and staghounds bay; the laughter and the silver speech of gay women and men float by with the bugle-calls on the breeze. But from all this brightness and music, which the poet's imagination conjures up, symbolizing the glitter and the indomitable energy of actual life, he turns back to the "shy recluses" whose world is the world of dreams and of consecration to the inner life. And so it is with Arnold again and again in his poetry; the fanfare of the present strikes dauntingly and with disillusioning power through the tender music of Romantic dreaming; the poet hears the insistent summons, but turns away half-fearfully, half-piously, toward the ideals of a less strenuous age.

Yet not even in his poetry is this Arnold's last word as to the worth of the world of everyday fact; nor is this his final imaginative appreciation of modern conventional life. The truth of the matter is that Romantic dreaming was for Arnold possible only in defiance of his conscience; the world of conventional fact had convicted him of sin, had imposed its claims upon him in spite of himself, and had made him feel that his duty lay in the acceptance of the commonplace and the fulfilment of everyday tasks. Accordingly, even in his poetry he substantially admits, as Clough admitted, that

E

"fact must be fact, and life the thing it can." His
acceptance of fact is never confident and grateful,
never very hopeful.   As he looks out on the modern world he has much to say of his "dwindling
faculty of joy"; of his soul which "perishes of
cold"; of a "weariness" which "no energy can
reach." He has much to say, too, of the unloveliness of the prospect that real life offers.   Our age
is "an iron time"; its wisdom is harshness; its
gayety is frivolity.   The world is made up of
"triflers," who amiably while life away, or of
slaves, who are dull victims of routine.   Yet this
world, unlovely as it is, is the world where, as
Wordsworth urged, men must find their happiness
or not at all.   The wise man will accept the conditions of life — will "submit, submit."   He must
not "fly to dreams," yet he need not despair.   He
will learn "to neither strive nor cry."   He will
train himself to that "wide and luminous view"
which substitutes for the petulance of individual
desire the calm and the resignation of philosophy.
He will open his soul to the temperate splendour
of nature and will steady himself through watching
and emulating her untroubled rhythms of achievement.   He will form himself in the spirit of her
"greatness," will "rally the good in the depths"
of himself, and "share in the world's toil."   His
faith in the ideal, he will retain as a kind of secret
life — a "Buried Life" — whence he may draw inspiration for his practical struggle with recalcitrant
reality.

Certainly there is nothing frolic or buoyant in this return of Arnold's to the regions of everyday fact. His home-coming almost suggests in its tempered meekness that of Goldsmith's Moses from the Fair with his famous gross of green spectacles. Yet Arnold has the pith of the matter in him; he accepts the laws of the great game of life. And though his mood, when compared with that of Browning or of Walt Whitman, may seem at the best a mood of finely controlled disheartenment, yet that there was much conscientious courage and stern endurance beneath what sometimes seems the pose of "weariness," his strenuous discharge through a long period of time of exasperatingly prosaic duties makes clear beyond the possibility of a query or a quibble.

During the last thirty years of his life, Arnold's medium of expression was almost wholly prose. His work during these years falls outside the period with which this essay is dealing, and is, moreover, in spirit and substance part and parcel of our modern age. This much, however, must at least be said of his prose — that alike in its origin and in its execution, it bears witness to his faith in the possibility of a reconciliation between the ideal and the real. His turning to prose may perhaps not too fantastically be regarded as his frank acceptance of conventional life with all its limitations. He turned to prose very much as Dipsychus finally submitted provisionally to the Power of this World.

"Welcome, O world, henceforth; and farewell dreams!" In the poem *Obermann once More*, there occurs a passage that seems meant by Arnold as an imaginative account of the purposes that guided him during his later life. The words are put into the mouth of the typical Romantic dreamer, Obermann, who in the poem appears to Arnold in visionary wise. He describes the hard, pitiless splendour of the pagan world, the passion of tenderness revealed in Christianity — in its Madonna-legend, its child-Christ, and its consolatory Man of Sorrows — the fervours of self-abnegation and of aspiring spirituality in Mediævalism, the pathetic dissolution of its dream-world and the defeat of its hopes and purposes. For Senancour, the Romantic age was the age of vain regret over the vanishing of delicate spirituality and the waning of mystical ardour; and there is much in Arnold's verse that tallies with this limited conception of the Romantic temper. Obermann describes the tumult of grieving and the bitter confusion of soul that overtook the men of his own age as they looked out upon a half-ruinous, half-recreated society in an era that had none of the spiritual or imaginative charm that their hearts exacted. And then he imposes upon his English follower the task of preserving for the men of the cruder modern age whatever he may of the beauty and the truth and the inspiriting power of mystical and Romantic ideals.

" Though more than half thy years be past,
    And spent thy youthful prime ;
Though round thy firmer manhood cast,
    Hang weeds of our sad time

" Whereof thy youth felt all the spell,
    And traversed all the shade —
Though late, though dimm'd, though weak, yet tell
    Hope to a world new-made ! "

And it was precisely to this task that Arnold
devoted himself in his prose-writings. He sought
to bring the real world into harmony, so far as he
might, with what seemed to his mature thought
best in Romantic ideals. He set himself with
rigorous and patient minuteness and unfaltering
ingenuity to a close struggle with the trivial and
prosaic details of actual life. He contended
against materialistic conceptions of life, against
"machinery," and against the worship of the favourite idols of a commercial and industrial age.
He sought to quicken in his fellows the life of the
spirit and to enlarge the range of their imaginations. He made familiar to Englishmen novel
ideas and novel points of view derived from abroad.
In every way he sought to increase the power of
spiritual and poetic ideals, always within the limits imposed by a sane regard for conventional
standards of thought and feeling and for the *common* sense. One is sometimes tempted to say im-
patiently that in his poetry Arnold's typical hero
is, after all, that philosophical poltroon Empedo-

cles who, in despair over the unloveliness of actual
life, flings himself headlong into a crater. Whether
or no this be a fair charge, certain it is that in his
prose criticism of life Arnold's model of all excellence, his lord and master, is Goethe, whose "large
and luminous view" he sought loyally to attain to,
and whose union of sane practicality with idealistic
fervour he recommends and emulates.

When we turn to Carlyle from Arnold we seem
going back to an earlier age. Carlyle is far more
audaciously loyal than Arnold to the idiom and the
manner of the idealists. In *Sartor Resartus* he at
times attacks the deadening power of custom and
convention with almost the virulence of the revolu-
tionists. Custom, he points out, makes "dotards"
of us all, subjects us to routine, victimizes us and
materializes us in countless ways. It is because
of his desire to free men from conventional blindness that in *Sartor Resartus* he makes such persistent and often such grotesque use of the famous
clothes-metaphor. He aims by the very grotesqueness of his imagery to shock men out of their
slavery to conventional ideas, to emancipate them
from the customary, to stir them to a fresh envisagement of the facts of life, to compel them to
realize that their beliefs, their religious forms and
creeds, their political institutions, their intellectual systems ought not to be adopted with the conventional nonchalance with which one accepts the
traditional and correct thing in hats and trousers.

In lieu of the materialistic and so-called common-
sense notions about man and life and the universe
that the ordinary Englishman unthinkingly contents himself with, Carlyle aims to substitute spiritual and even mystical conceptions. He would
replace, or at any rate supplement, eighteenth-
century sound sense with German transcendentalism. He quotes from that fierce realist, Swift, a
definition of man, — "a forked, straddling animal
with bandy legs," — and adds, "yet also a Spirit,
and unutterable Mystery of Mysteries." This is
typical of Carlyle's method and aim. He was the
first Englishman to deal victoriously in widely
read prose with that fallacious and cynical distrust
of genius and imagination and of all the more mysterious elements in human nature which had ruled
English thought and literature since at least the
days of Swift.

Carlyle's transcendentalism, as expounded in
Sartor Resartus, is, of course, nowadays an old and
somewhat discredited story. Transcendentalism
is apt to seem to the modern mind simply one of
the beautiful vagaries of a web-spinning age. Yet
very beautiful it still is as one follows its elabora-
tion in Carlyle's richly imaginative dialect. And
by more than one generation of readers it has been
welcomed with the utmost eagerness as a prevailing
defence against those mechanical theories of the
universe that so thrive among English Philistines.
For Carlyle, the only two realities in the universe

are the Divine Will and the Human Will. Nature
is a mass of beautiful sensuous symbols whereby
God speaks to the human soul. The world is "but
an air-image." Man's body is "dust and shadow;
a shadow-system gathered round our Me, wherein,
through some moments or years, the Divine Essence is to be revealed in the Flesh." Laws,
religious beliefs and ceremonies, artistic methods,
political institutions, are merely the spiritual forms
through which man's ceaseless striving for ideal
ends records its progress and seeks to make this
progress continuous and permanent; their dwelling
is in the mind of man, and their life from generation to generation is a spiritual life. Cities, tilled
fields, books — these, too, are but treasuries in
which infinite spiritual energy has been stored
through the past experience of the race. "So
spiritual is our whole daily Life; all that we do
springs out of Mystery, Spirit, invisible Force;
only like a little Cloud-image, or Armida's Palace,
air-built, does the Actual body itself forth from
the great mystic Deep." And so Carlyle's imagination ranges far and wide among the records of
civilization, through the regions of nature, over the
revolving earth-ball, and throughout the Cosmos,
finding underneath material disguises spiritual energy everywhere in play. He unbuilds the
seemingly solid frame of the universe and dissolves
its base corporeal substance; he refines away all
perturbing alloy until he reveals everywhere the

pulsing energy of pure spirit, Human Power and
Divine Power weaving tirelessly the fabric of
existence.

Yet in spite of all his magniloquent dreaming,
Carlyle is true, or means to be true, to the uncom-
promising facts of life; he dreams only that he
may the more victoriously labour; and in his Gospel of Work and his doctrine of Hero-worship he
returns from the misty regions of transcendentalism and confronts the practical concerns of common
life. No one is more contemptuous than Carlyle
of dilettante web-spinning or of idle playing with
emotion. Byron's egoistic woe, he scorns and
ridicules. One of his mandates in *Sartor Resartus*
is "Close thy Byron; open thy Goethe." "What
if thou wert born and predestined not to be Happy,
but to be Unhappy! Art thou nothing other than
a Vulture, then, that fliest through the Universe
seeking after somewhat to *eat;* and shrieking dole-
fully because carrion enough is not given thee?"
All the private, individual grieving which the Romanticists had so plangently or so delicately and
picturesquely phrased for the delectation of their
age, Carlyle contemns. He sends the laggard
euphuist back to actual life, and bids him forget
himself and his fine words in some practical task.
"There is endless hope in work." "'Tools and
the Man' — that, henceforth to all time, is now
our Epic." "Do the Duty which lies nearest thee."
In these principles and precepts, Carlyle reveals a

practical, ethical interest not to be found in such purely Romantic prose-writers as Lamb, Hazlitt, and De Quincey; and by virtue of this new and decisive interest he belongs to the later or post-Romantic age. He is not primarily an imaginative artist, not a mere dreamer; he insists that dreams be realized in the hard, unmalleable stuff of life. His "Heroes" are simply the workers who thus victoriously embody their dreams in solid fact. Mahomet, Dante, Luther, Cromwell, — they all saw beyond the conventional shows of things; they were all seers or dreamers; but they were also more than dreamers, and triumphantly brought their dreams to pass in some portion or other of the recalcitrant material of daily life. Carlyle's Hero is the Deformed Romanticist Transformed into a heroic worker of results. His last word to beautifully complaining visionaries is a charge that they immerse themselves in the Actual: "Yes here, in this poor, miserable, hampered, despicable Actual, wherein thou even now standest, here or nowhere is thy Ideal: work it out therefrom; and working, believe, live, be free. Fool! the Ideal is in thyself, the impediment too is in thyself: thy Condition is but the stuff thou art to shape that same Ideal out of; what matters whether such stuff be of this sort or that, so the Form thou give it be heroic, be poetic?"

On the need, then, of a synthesis between the Actual and the Ideal, Carlyle insists with much

gorgeous rhetoric. But if he be asked for definite
and close suggestions about this synthesis, his
answers are apt to be vague or even impatient.
"Let not any Parliament Member ask of this
Editor, What is to be done? . . . Editors are not
here, foremost of all, to say How. . . . An Editor's stipulated work is to apprise *thee* that it must
be done. The 'way to do it' — is to try it, knowing that thou shalt die if it be not done." This is
both ungracious and tantalizingly elusive. But its
vagueness is characteristic of the whole post-Romantic attitude toward conventional life. After
all, the post-Romanticists were not passionately
enough in love with the Actual to follow out its
facts and their laws with patient fidelity through
all their complications and variations. They saw
life and they loved life in its large contours, in its
pageantry, under its more moving and more typical
aspects. They lacked the microscopic eye and the
ingenious instinct for detail that are characteristic
of the modern artist and of the modern commen-
tator on life. It remained for the scientific spirit
with its fine loyalty to fact, and for realism with
its delicate sense of the worth of the passing
moment — of the *phase* — to carry still further
the return to the regions of the Actual.

TENNYSON'S RELATION TO COMMON LIFE

TENNYSON's poetry passes decisively beyond that of Clough, Mrs. Browning, and Matthew Arnold in its reaction against Romanticism. Earlier than any of these poets Tennyson recognized in verse the dangers of lonely Romantic dreaming. The *Palace of Art*, first published in 1833, portrays in richly ornate allegory the mental and moral disasters that are apt to overtake the dilettante who isolates himself from his fellows in the pursuit of beauty. It seems almost a prophecy of what later befell Dante Gabriel Rossetti and a poetical diagnosis of his morbidness and maladies. It may justly be taken as expressing once for all Tennyson's unswerving conviction that an artist, in order both to preserve his normality and to give his art its widest scope and most vital power, must keep in close sympathy with the common life of his time. The recluse dreamer that Tennyson portrays in the poem is the typical Romantic Wanderer, fallen heir to a fortune and endowed with a sense of ways and means. He builds his soul a lordly pleasure-house, gathers into it all forms and objects of art that may minister to

60

a nobly passionate search for visionary beauty, and
devotes himself in the midst of these new and
exquisitely directed conditions to the old Romantic
quest after the ideal. But, as every one remembers, bad dreams force themselves upon him
through all his safeguards and mar the calculated
perfection of his visionary world; he is tortured
with strange fancies; he feels the bonds of
sane self-possession dissolving; the universe seems
closing in upon him impalpably and terribly, —
destroying with its threats the tranquil and harmonious movement of his imaginative life. And
so he at last abandons his many-chambered palace
of dreams, and goes down to make his abode in " a
cottage in the vale," where he may draw solace
and strength from " the common heart and need."
To Tennyson, isolated dreaming, even though one
yield to it under the most exquisite and least sensuous conditions, seems bound to prove futile and
disastrous.

But though Tennyson thus early and decisively condemned the waywardness and the remoteness of Romanticism, his own manner of life
was curiously unaccordant. He was himself less
reconciled with the conventionalities, less at home
in the world of sheer fact, than perhaps any other
great poet of his day. From first to last, in his
relations with his fellow men, he was wilful,
almost grotesque, in his maintenance of the pose of
the special soul. In bearing, dress, and manner he

was singular, picturesque, irreducible to rule. He
wore all the forms of life with a somewhat challenging difference. He had none of Browning's
frank interest in the routine of society; he guarded
for himself a kind of splendid privacy; he shut
himself away from the dulness or the clamour of
commonplace life in the beautiful wood-girdled
fastness of Farringford, or in the heart of the
heather in the Surrey hills at Aldworth. Of course,
the whole world knows the greatness of the man,
his flawless sincerity, and the scope and largeness
of his nature; there was in him no strain of little-
ness, no taint of affectation. And so the slight, but
persistent, strangeness of his movement among his
fellows must be accepted as the genuine and necessary expression of peculiarities of temperament,
which made it impossible for him to conventionalize
himself without harming what was quintessential
in his nature.

Throughout Tennyson's art there run traces of
this same inconsistency between theory and practice. Theoretically, he was convinced of the imperative need of a synthesis between the actual
and the ideal, and of the incontrovertible claims
of commonplace life and the conventional world of
organized society. Law, order, coöperative effort,
— these conceptions are in his verse everywhere
exalted. The individual is tutored into subjection
to the rights of the body politic. Wellington and
King Arthur — his typical heroes — are men whose

natures are through and through wrought into obedience to law. The ideal of the State calls forth Tennyson's passionate devotion, and often stirs his imagination into the creation of fervent beauty. He is conspicuously patriotic, and is indeed almost insular in his keen loyalty to English traditions, English habits of life, English religious ideas, English landscapes, and the British Constitution. Under this Constitution, he finds reconciled as nowhere else, passion for individual freedom and reverence for order, and he celebrates the Constitution as the symbol of the marvellous English genius for self-government; he finds treasured up in it the results of long generations of strenuous, but controlled, effort after more perfect social adjustment. He sings of England as,

> " A land of settled government,
> A land of just and old renown,
> Where Freedom slowly broadens **down**
> From precedent to precedent."

Tennyson's fervid patriotism and his ardent exaltation of order distinguish him from most of the great poets of the century: from the rebels, Byron and Shelley, whose tirades against English tyranny were notoriously fierce; and also from Clough and Arnold, whose love of country was tempered with much philosophic doubt.

In his relations to science, too, Tennyson is **far** more modern than Clough or Arnold; here also he

shows an increased closeness to fact and a striving
to reconcile, at least theoretically, the world of
fact with the world of dreams. The purpose of *In
Memoriam* is, of course, from first to last to bring
about this reconciliation. The poem sets itself to
envisage unflinchingly under all its aspects the
commonest and ugliest fact of human existence —
death. It keeps continually in view the most
discouraging conclusions that the scientific intellect urges about man's base origin, about nature's
indifference to man's destiny, and about the in-
significance of the human drama as a part of the
great cosmic process. Yet the poet wins to beauty
through all this adversity; he brings sweetness out
of the bitterness of death; he convinces at least the
heart that the grief and the tragedy of actual life
are not absolute evil.

In such poems as these, then, and in such ways
as these,— through insistence by means of picturesque symbols on the intimate relation of art to life
and through a lyrical outpouring of personal conviction as regards the worth of life, — Tennyson at-
tempts a reconciliation of the actual with the ideal.
In so far he has got the better of the detachment
that is characteristic of Romantic poetry.

But when we go beyond his theories of life and
his lyrical poems, and question how far he can veri-
tably lay hold of the world of everyday experience
and reproduce it in his art visibly and audibly, so
that it shall have perfect truth of detail and yet

a redeeming glamour, then we become aware of
the limitations of his genius, and are once more
troubled by that shrinking from the commonplace
and from the crude, and by that monopolizing interest in subjective emotion, which have already
been noted as characteristic of him as a man.
With the actual drama of human life Tennyson
cannot cope; he cannot redeem its triviality; he
cannot bring beauty out of its turmoil and confusion; he cannot interpret into fine significance its
puzzling complexities of motive, character, and
passionate action. He cannot vanquish the repel-
lent imperfections and defects of actual experience,
and show, in the unwrought dross and tortured
material of commonplace existence, God in the
making; he cannot reveal God in the passing
hours. For this kind of renovating imaginative
realism he lacks courage; he lacks also the necessary frank hospitality toward all kinds of experience, the quick insight into motive and character,
and the wide and close familiarity with the drama
of life.

External nature he can reproduce with what
seems like truth and yet with beauty, for here he
can be selective and subjective. But when he
uses these same capricious methods for the treatment of character and conduct, his poetry comes
perilously near taking on Romantic falseness of
tone and substance; and it is this falsification of
actual life that is meant when Tennyson is spoken

F

of as still under the sway of Romantic moods, as still using Romantic methods.

In considering these limitations of Tennyson's genius as affecting his relation to actual life, the *Idylls of the King* and other narrative poems that deal with legendary subjects may at once be set aside. In such poems Tennyson confessedly gives himself over to remote and beautiful dreaming. The dramas, too, may be neglected; these are by universal consent unreal, unconvincing, lyrically beautiful, but weak in characterization and untrue. There remain two classes of poems that profess to treat common and contemporary life sincerely and yet imaginatively: first, poems that may be called Idylls of Rustic Life, such poems as *Dora* and the *Gardener's Daughter;* here, too, belongs *Enoch Arden:* secondly, poems that take their subjects and characters direct from the artificial world of conventional society; the most important of these poems are *Locksley Hall* and the monodrama, *Maud.*

Tennyson's relation to actual life in poems of the first class may be illustrated from *Enoch Arden.* Walter Bagehot has in one of his essays briefly pointed out how remote this poem continually keeps from the world of fact. Never for a moment in *Enoch Arden* is the reader brought into touch with real characters or with the real experiences of sailors. What the poem does is to put before the reader with exquisite deftness what such characters and such experiences become as they pass through

the dreamy mind and before the visionary imagination of the poet who wrote the *Lady of Shalott*
and *Tears, idle tears.* The poem has none of the
savour of fact. It is lyrically falsified from first
to last— qualified into grace and music through the
poet's refinement of temperament. An excellent
illustration of this lyrical falsification is to be
found in the description of Enoch on the desert
island: —

" The mountain wooded to the peak, the lawns
    And winding glades high up like ways to Heaven,
    The slender coco's drooping crown of plumes,
    The lightning flash of insect and of bird,
    The lustre of the long convolvuluses
    That coil'd around the stately stems, and ran
    Ev'n to the limit of the land, the glows
    And glories of the broad belt of the world,
    All these he saw ; but what he fain had seen
    He could not see, the kindly human face,
    Nor ever hear a kindly voice, but heard
    The myriad shriek of wheeling ocean-fowl,
    The league-long roller thundering on the reef,
    The moving whisper of huge trees that branch'd
    And blossom'd in the zenith, or the sweep
    Of some precipitous rivulet to the wave,
    As down the shore he ranged, or all day long
    Sat often in the seaward-gazing gorge,
    A shipwreck'd sailor, waiting for a sail :
    No sail from day to day, but every day
    The sunrise broken into scarlet shafts
    Among the palms and ferns and precipices ;
    The blaze upon the waters to the east ;
    The blaze upon his island overhead ;
    The blaze upon the waters to the west ;
    Then the great stars that globed themselves in Heaven,

> The hollower-bellowing ocean, and again
> The scarlet shafts of sunrise — but no sail."

The splendour and the beauty of these lines, their
imaginative power, are beyond cavil; but what they
really convey to us is Tennyson's lyrical comment
on Enoch's isolation, not for a moment a vivid, vital
sense of Enoch's own actual appreciation of his
fate. Fancy Robinson Crusoe trying to find his
mind mirrored in Tennyson's rhodomontade.

There is no truth in the psychology of Enoch;
he is a sentimental, soft-hearted dreamer. There
is no truth in the emotional atmosphere through
which the background of minor characters and of
nature is shown to us. The whole story is conceived in sentiment and brought forth in melodious
lyricism. As a plea, therefore, for the essential
worth of common life the poem has no constraining
power. We feel persistently that the charm and
the glamour come not from life itself, but from the
temperament and the technique of the poet. We
cannot be made in love with life by the delicate
imagery and the musical cadences of this tale of
self-sacrifice. There is no genuine synthesis of
the actual and the ideal; for the poet shows no
firm grasp on the actual. The sailor he describes
is anæmic and semi-hysterical; the refinements of
the sailor's spiritual struggle are highly improb-
able; the returning wanderer would far more likely
have conducted himself as Guy de Maupassant's

seaman did in *Le Retour*. Finally, even if characters and incidents and atmosphere all seemed
true, the poem would, nevertheless, because of the
faint-heartedness of the sentiment, not be a successful renovation of life; it would be more apt to give
the reader a fit of the spleen than to send him out
frankly and willingly into the world to take what
it offers.

When we turn to the second group of poems that
portray actual life, we find Tennyson's Romantic
proclivities no less in evidence, although revealing
themselves in a new fashion. In *Maud*, a typical
poem of this class, the author's own personality
less obviously interposes a false atmosphere between the reader and actual life. But the falsification nevertheless exists, and Tennyson's inability
to re-create the commonplace in terms of beauty
shows itself as unmistakably as ever. The whole
poem is the overwrought, half-frenzied dream of
a mind diseased,— the mind of the hero, whose
ideas and feelings and fancies make up the substance of the poem, and through whose eyes and
morbid temperament we are continually forced to
look at whatever happens. This hero is the son of
a suicide; he has a bias toward insanity; he has
been all his days a lonely, myopic, inconsolable
misanthrope; he inveighs much and often against
the common lot and his own individual fate; he
kills a man in a duel,— the brother of the woman he
loves; he is separated from his betrothed and goes

mad. Finally, after suffering from various hallucinations, he gets back his reason; and he escapes
from his private woe through going for a soldier.

All this may be contemporary, but it certainly is
not common life, and it certainly *is* morbid. The
undeniable beauty of the poem is won through the
help of a madman. To seem to Tennyson worth
portrayal, the actual life of the present has to
be edited in terms of the mind and the imagination
of a monomaniac. Once more, then, Tennyson,
though he professedly concerns himself with a
subject drawn from the life around him, fails to
bring about any satisfactory synthesis of the ideal
and the actual. The piece of actual life that
attracts his imagination is too unusual and strange
to be representative; and the mode of portrayal,
though true to the hero's temper, completely falsifies
the values of normal existence. Moreover, the
poem ends with a curious Romantic flourish; the
hero rushes off to fight for his country. Only in
the pageantry and the excitement of war can he
hope to forget his selfish passion and despair.
The poem seems almost like a survival from the
period of storm and stress.

But besides the unreality of his narrative poems,
there are several minor ways in which Tennyson's
Romantic discomfort in the presence of actual life
shows itself. He is fond of allegory, and this fondness is perhaps a sign of his powerlessness over the
actual stuff of life, — of his inability to give us

with accuracy and yet with beauty the contours and
the configurations and the rugged aspects of the
world of fact. He likes to build his own cosmos
of truth, instead of finding and revealing God's
truth in God's cosmos. He delights in fashioning
beautiful stories in which personified abstractions
or simplified typical characters are the actors, and
in which some theory or set of impressive ideas is
symbolically illustrated. In the *Palace of Art* he
demonstrates abstractly the dangers of dilettantism; in the *Vision of Sin* he shows in a splendid
and terrible pageant the pleasures and the pains
of wickedness; the *Idylls of the King* are throughout conceived and executed in accordance with
an allegorical design. This instinct in an artist
toward the region of allegorical abstractions is apt
to go along with a shrinking dislike of the stark
facts of actual life. The artist withdraws from
the turmoil of the real universe into the fortress of
his own mind, and beats the enemy in toy battles
with toy soldiers. He demonstrates on maps and
on paper that the devil must at last get the worst
of it in the world.

The same lack of control over concrete facts
shows itself in the shallowness and vagueness of
Tennyson's characterization. The men and the
women in his lyrics and his narratives have no
minutely realized individualities; they are of interest to Tennyson because of the moods and the
dreams they suggest to him; they do not tempt

him into close analysis of their minds and hearts, of the peculiar interplay of their moods, motives, and acts; indeed, as conceived by Tennyson they rarely have any complex inner life of thought and feeling. Sometimes they are types, — characters simplified for a moral purpose; sometimes, as in the *Idylls*, they are effective figures in romantic stories of love and war, and their acts flow directly and simply from elemental desires and passions, and express the somewhat conventional qualities of brave knights and fair ladies.   But whatever the special value for Tennyson of the men and the women in his poems, they do not challenge him to subtle psychological studies, of the sort, for example, that Browning delights in.   The actual facts of the inner lives of men and women have little interest or fascination for him; he cares hardly more for these inner facts than for the actual outward facts of everyday existence.   His own moods and his own dreams are what he instinctively watches and interprets.   Characters are worth while according to their power to excite rare moods of reverie and exquisite dreams.   Tennyson is little better than a lotos-eater in his interpretation of character.

Tennyson's curious self-involvement in the presence of the personalities he watches or creates, his lack of vital dramatic sympathy and insight, are well illustrated in the series of poems that bear the names of women, — *Lilian, Isabel, Madeline, Eleä-nore, Adeline,* and *Margaret.*   About each of these

fair women Tennyson " dreams deliciously"; each
is " made one with nature," is portrayed through
beautiful symbols drawn from landscape and forest
and hillside and "the blue regions of the air. "
But *what* is portrayed? Not a mind and an intricate character, but a peculiar type of beauty
(involving a temperament, to be sure), as the type
plays luxuriously upon the moods and the imagination of the poet.

> " How may full-sail'd verse express,
> How may measured words adore
> The full-flowing harmony
> Of thy swan-like stateliness,
> Eleänore ?
> The luxuriant symmetry
> Of thy floating gracefulness,
> Eleänore ?
> Every turn and glance of thine,
> Every lineament divine,
> Eleänore,
> And the steady sunset glow,
> That stays upon thee ? "

This is very beautiful, but it is certainly not
psychology. Nor is there a subtler interpretation
of character in *Fatima, Œnone,* and the two *Mari-
anas;* they are merely studies of passion in terms
of landscape. The picturesque aspects of character are what interest Tennyson, not the subtleties
or the intricacies of mind and heart. This lack
of psychological truth is only one more illustration
of Tennyson's lack of instinct for the actual, — of

his remoteness from the common lot, — of his half-romantic subjectivity, — of his preoccupation with the dream or with his own moods.

In all these ways, then, and for all these reasons, Tennyson fails of perfect imaginative control of common life, comes short of being a renovating interpreter of the commonplace. The truth of the matter is, that he had no vital faith in the commonplace such as Browning had, or belief in its essential worth. He was undemocratic in every fibre of his delicate recluse nature. He does his utmost in his art to be loyal to his age, to the wearisome tracts of the trivial in human life, even to the claims of the ugly and to the rights of pain and sin. He succeeds in theoretically justifying to himself all these repulsive elements in the universe as part of some divinely guided process which shall ultimately lead to crowning good. The closing lines of *In Memoriam* express the poet's belief in

> "One far-off divine event
> To which the whole creation moves."

Yet this very confession of faith is, after all, an illustration of Tennyson's distrust and dislike of the present. In the actual moment he is unable to find redeeming beauty or worth; he can regard the passing moment, the welter of good and evil that he looks out upon, as worth while only as it may be atoned for by some far-away excellence to-

ward which it is groping.   The present he tolerates
simply as it contains the promise and potency
of some remote future.   This is merely, in a more
refined form, the old Romantic blasphemy against
life and the spirit that informs it.   Greater faith,
greater heartiness, more courage than this, are
needed in a poet; otherwise he can hardly hope
to portray a fragment of our actual fleeting life
so as to make it seem divinely significant in spite
of all its apparent triviality and its undeniable
grossness and ugliness.

Finally, even when Tennyson renders some piece
of actual life exquisite in its appeal to us, the
charm too often seems something adventitious,
something artificially added to life, not resident in
life and simply revealed by the poet.   The beauty,
for example, in *Enoch Arden* seems distilled into
the story from the poet's temperament through the
aid of musical rhythms and delicately wrought
imagery.   This is the old dubious method of
Romanticism to which long ago Jeffrey and Peacock
narrowly and unintelligently objected and in which
later criticism has more precisely noted the eccentricity and untrustworthiness.   Romantic poets —
so the charge runs — give us their capricious
moods about life; they show us life with the em-
bellishment imparted to it by their quaintly iridescent temperaments.   They give us a report, not of
some actual region of fact, but of the mirage
thereof cast against the heavens by the haze of

intense emotion in the midst of which they are perpetually moving and breathing. What they have to offer is news of the state of the emotional atmosphere, not news of the rugged earth. Their ideal is a visionary ideal in the clouds; the actual remains below unredeemed. The beauty of the mirage, we come often to feel, is an artificial affair, the product of the refractions of personal feeling, of the individual horizon, of the evanescent lights and colours of poetic imagery, and of the shaping winds of rhythm. Beauty of this kind is worth while; yet it is in some degree accidental and abnormal; it is in very truth only exquisite feigning. Tennyson in his imaginative treatment of actual life fails for the most part to create beauty more essential or permanent than this, or beauty that is more organically and necessarily related to common experience. He has still something of the visionary blindness of Romanticism when he tries to move about in the midst of the trivial incident and the varying turmoil of daily life. Out of what his vision has vouchsafed him, he creates lyrical poetry of irresistible sweetness and beauty. But his eye, while he has been watching the splendours of dreamland, has not learned the aspect or the meaning of the commonplace, and he makes his way uncertainly through a world that he only partially realizes.

NATURE IN TENNYSON'S POETRY

ONE of the most important effects of the Romantic movement was the closeness of the relation it established between nature and the human soul. The intense and oftentimes eccentric emotions that tended to throw the Romantic poet out of sympathy with his fellow men and with conventional life became the solvent of the rigid forms of the material universe. The poet's fervid mood proved the very fire necessary to fuse nature once and for all with emotion, to make it coalesce with thought and the inner life of man, and to unite matter and spirit more subtly and intimately than ever before. The Romantic poets subdued nature to spirit; they interpreted nature in terms of human feeling; they sent their imaginations out along countless lines of subtle association, drew all nature into sympathy with their intense experiences, and converted all the facts and forms of nature into "the passion-wingèd ministers of thought." Nature was no longer to stand apart from man as a system of half-hostile forces, or a mass of dry facts, meaningless except for science: it was not to be as for Pope and the Deists merely a great machine of infinitely ingenious construction, set running once and for all

by the great Mechanician and for ever after grind-
ing out effects unerringly and inevitably.   For
many Romantic poets — notably for Wordsworth,
Coleridge, and Shelley — nature was a direct emana-
tion from the one great spiritual force which mani-
fests itself also in the myriad individuals that make
up the human race. The countless ideas and feelings that float through the mind of man and the
countless shapes and aspects of the world of nature
were alike the utterance of one great imaginative
Artist, who expressed through these two sets of
symbols his thoughts of beauty and truth. Hence
the poet who seeks a proper image to stand for his
thought has simply to let his imagination guide him
through the beautiful forms of nature till he finds
a fitting symbol; his thoughts are God's thoughts,
and have been already uttered in some fixed shape
of beauty, or through some changing aspect, of
the outside world. This is really the postulate
on which Wordsworth's and Coleridge's theory
of imagination depends; imagination, they urge
leads to objective truth, while fancy only plays
prettily with images ; imagination discerns essential
analogies between mind and matter, and brings once
more into at least transient unity the world of spirit
and the world of nature.

Tennyson's poetry carries on with fine loyalty
and in some ways with increased effectiveness the
Romantic tradition in the treatment of nature. Not
that he accepts or expresses extreme transcendental

conceptions of the relation of nature to man and of nature and man to God. The scientific spirit is continually imposing its check upon him and compelling him to recognize, at least transiently, the literal meaning of the facts of nature as interpreted by the analytic, positive mind of his day and generation. Yet the Romantic mood of intimacy with nature survives in Tennyson, not simply undiscouraged by the revelations of science, but even quickened and intensified in its delicate susceptibility. He has done more than perhaps any other single poet of this century to spiritualize nature in the sense of making it subservient to the needs of the human soul and of forcing it to become symbolical of human moods and passions. He has done even more than Wordsworth to give a new meaning to nature; for whereas Wordsworth worked continually in the interests of a few simple moods with which many men nowadays cannot fully sympathize, Tennyson has had at his service an exquisitely graduated temperament, varying through an almost limitless range of complex moods, nearly every one of which may be shared by a sensitive reader.

From the outset Tennyson's poetry was noteworthy for its powerful and suggestive use of landscape. *Mariana* in his first volume, and *Mariana in the South, Fatima,* and *Œnone* in his second volume were experiments after effects not before attempted in English literature. These poems are not studies of different "ways of love," or merely

portraits of different types of women; they are im-
mensely imaginative studies of irresistible and all-
dominating moods, each of which is symbolized
through the figure of a woman portrayed against a
sympathetic background of nature. They are studies of landscape as landscape is seen through an
atmosphere determined by feeling. Each poem
owes its power to the congruity of its details, to the
imaginative unity that pervades it and subdues
every minutest circumstance of colour and light and
shade and motion till they all breathe out one inevitable chord of feeling. The blinding light and
the stifling heat of the landscapes in *Mariana in
the South* seem the very exhalation of defeated
passion; in the other *Mariana*, the details of the
"lonely moated grange," from the "blackest moss"
of the flower-plots to the "glooming flats" and
"dark fens," all image *Mariana's* deadly languor
and desolation. The poem is a study in black of a
passion of melancholy as the other poem is a study
in flame-colours of a passion of consuming tenderness and devotion.

Of course, there are not many of the poems that
have such absolute imaginative unity. But there
is a second group where noticeably similar effects
are gained by somewhat similar methods; this
group contains most of the other poems that are
called by the names of women, — *Lilian, Isabel,
Madeline, Eleänore, Adeline,* and *Margaret.* Each
poem portrays a temperament in terms of look,

gesture, bearing, complexion, and form; each is the interpretation of a woman's soul as it reveals itself by means of subtle material symbols. The power of each poem is due to the poet's intuitive appreciation of the value of material facts as the expression of thought and feeling. Two of the poems, *Adeline* and *Margaret*, beside portraying typical women, have a symbolical value; the "twin-sisters" symbolize the Romantic spirit as it shows itself now in the fanciful interpretation of nature, and now in the deeply imaginative interpretation of the passionate life of past generations. The less human of the sisters, "shadowy, dreaming Adeline," weaves into bright and tender myths all she sees in the outside world; she dreams childlike dreams over butter-flies, bluebells, and "lilies at dawn," and finds all nature instinct with half-fantastic life. Margaret is the type of the Romantic spirit in its more serious moods and its "more human" sympathies; of its passion for "dainty sorrow" and of its ardent reveries over the great deeds and glorious tragedies of history.

> " What can it matter, Margaret,
>   What songs below the waning stars
> The lion-heart, Plantagenet,
>   Sang looking thro' his prison bars ?
>   Exquisite Margaret, who can tell
>   The last wild thought of Chatelet,
> Just ere the falling axe did part
> The burning brain from the true heart,
>   Even in her sight he loved so well."

G

Thoughts and images like these are the "feast of sorrow" from which the pale lady of Romance is loath to part. The mood that is suggested is much like that of Keats's more sombre odes; it has much in common with the mood of those verses which in the *Ode to a Nightingale* describe Ruth "amid the alien corn." Both passages send the imagination travelling back along the dark ways of history to the intense passionate experience of an isolated soul; both depend for their effectiveness on the curious modern mood that finds a special charm in the uncertain lights and shades, the mysterious chiaroscuro of the past.

The other poems of this group probably have no symbolical meaning; but they are quite as remarkable for their portrayal of temperament through bodily signs. And the interesting point to be noted with reference to all these poems is that they form one more illustration of the far-reaching sensitiveness to harmonies between matter and spirit which is perhaps in the last analysis the deepest source of Tennyson's power.

Besides the poems of the two general groups already considered, there are, of course, many others in Tennyson's earliest volumes which contain atmospheric landscapes of remarkable beauty and suggestiveness. In the *Ode to Memory* there occurs a series of landscapes which are called up out of the poet's boyhood; and they all have the dewy splendour, the freshness, the brilliancy of the

impressions of youth; there rests on all of them the
light of early morning. The *Lotos-Eaters* portrays
a series of scenes from the land where "it seemed
always afternoon"; the poem is a study in yellow
and gold and orange; the landscapes are seen
through a dreamy mellow haze and in the light of a
westering sun; and not one of them could be conceived of as occurring in the *Ode to Memory*. Nor
could the following landscape be found by any
possibility in the *Lotos-Eaters:* —

> " Pour round my ears the livelong bleat
>   Of the thick-fleeced sheep from wattled folds,
>   Upon the ridged wolds,
>   When the first matin-song hath waken'd loud
>   Over the dark dewy earth forlorn,
>   What time the amber morn
>   Forth gushes from beneath a low-hung cloud."

There breathe through these lines the sense of mystery and the awe and yet the hope and the keen
delight that are stirred in the heart of an impres-
sionable boy by the sights and sounds of dawn.
The Lotos-Eaters knew no such nature as this.

Nor is it only in Tennyson's early or short poems
that this atmospheric treatment of landscape is to
be found. His later long narrative poems are full of
equally good illustrations of his power to re-create
nature in terms of a dominating mood. The action
of these poems goes on in the midst of natural
scenery which is perpetually varying in tone and
colour, and light and shade, in sympathy with the

mood of the moment. In *Maud*, this suffusion of
nature with passion is especially noticeable; and
the hysterics and bad psychology of that poem are
made endurable by the beauty of such imaginative
sketches as the following : —

"I heard no sound where I stood
  But the rivulet on from the lawn
  Running down to my own dark wood ;
  Or the voice of the long sea-wave as it swell'd
  Now and then in the dim-gray dawn ;
  But I look'd, and round, all round the house I beheld
  The death-white curtain drawn ;
  Felt a horror over me creep,
  Prickle my skin and catch my breath,
  Knew that the death-white curtain meant but sleep,
  Yet I shudder'd and thought like a fool of the sleep of
      death."

This should be compared with Wordsworth's
"Strange fits of passion have I known"; the mood
is substantially the same; but Tennyson's lines are
far finer in phrasing, more suggestive in imagery,
and more thoroughly atmospheric.

In *Enoch Arden*, too, there are many passages
where, with like intensity and imaginative power,
nature is subdued to the passion of the moment.
What could be finer from this point of view or more
inappropriate from the point of view of Enoch's
psychology than the famous lines describing
Enoch's sense of isolation on the desert island ? —

"No sail from day to day, but every day
  The sunrise broken into scarlet shafts

Among the palms and ferns and precipices ;
The blaze upon the waters to the east ;
The blaze upon his island overhead ;
The blaze upon the waters to the west ;
Then the great stars that globed themselves in **Heaven,**
The hollower-bellowing ocean, and again
The scarlet shafts of sunrise — but no sail."

In order to bring out more unmistakably the
peculiar transformation to which in such descriptions as these nature submits in passing through
Tennyson's temperament, it may be well to quote
two or three of his simpler descriptions of natural
scenery where he merely portrays frankly and
delicately some clearly visualized aspect or object
of the outside world.   Descriptions of this sort also
abound, and are wrought out with an exquisite fineness of detail that does not preclude breadth of
treatment, and with marvellous felicity of phrase.
The first of the following passages is from *Margaret*
and the second from *Maud :* —

> " The sun is just about to set,
>   The arching limes are tall and shady,
>   And faint, rainy lights are seen,
>   Moving in the leavy beech."

> " I was walking a mile,
>   More than a mile from the shore,
>   The sun look'd out with a smile
>   Betwixt the cloud and the moor,
>   And riding at set of day
>   Over the dark moor land,
>   Rapidly riding far away,
>   She waved to me with her hand.

There were two at her side,
Something flash'd in the sun,
Down by the hill I saw them ride,
In a moment they were gone."

The lines from *Margaret* show as loving and faithful a study of nature as Wordsworth's, and as great delicacy of phrase in recording unusual or little noticed aspects of the outside world. The passage from *Maud* is a masterpiece of description; the landscape is sketched, in its broad features, with bold, free strokes, and the figures are flashed upon the reader's imagination by a gleam of light and a motion. In both these passages the treatment is sincere and simple; nature is shown under a white light, with no modifying or harmonizing atmosphere. But description of this kind, though attractive enough in its way and bearing witness to the perfection of Tennyson's technique, lacks the specific charm and peculiar power of Romantic description; it is not imaginative in the distinctively Romantic meaning of the term; it does not, to use Lamb's words, "draw all things to one." In the passages earlier considered, the unifying and harmonizing power of imagination pervades every line, phrase, and word, and makes them all eloquent of a single thought and mood. This action of imagination is compared by Wordsworth in a famous passage of the last book of the *Prelude*, to the light of the moon as this light is seen, from the summit of a lofty hill, falling on a widespread landscape, and blending all the infinitely various details into a single harmonious impression of splendour and power.

Such Romantic imagination in dealing with nature Tennyson possessed in a high degree; and indeed, from one point of view, he may be said simply to have carried on to richer conclusions the work which the Romanticists began. As has already been suggested, he has probably been more influential than even Wordsworth, in conveying widely and permanently into the English temperament a delicate and swiftly responsive sensitiveness to the emotional suggestiveness of nature. Wordsworth was, in large measure, preoccupied with the moral meaning of the external world; to quote his own words, he sought "to exhibit the most ordinary appearances of the material universe under moral relations." Tennyson subdues nature still further and makes it eloquent of all our moods and passions. Wordsworth's moods are comparatively limited in variety and in subtlety; their very grandeur and their lofty elevation, when Wordsworth is at his best, prevent great refinement or great subtlety of feeling. His temperament is too simple, and his nature has too great mass, to admit of complex combinations of feelings or of quick and ravishing changes. "Admiration, love, and awe," these are the moods Wordsworth most insists on; and in the service of these cogent but comparatively simple feelings he is fondest of interpreting the great world of nature. Tennyson's moods, on the other hand,

run through a very wide range and shade into each
other through an infinite series of gradations. He
plays on an instrument of far greater delicacy of
adjustment and of much greater variety of tone-
colour. He was heir to all the rich emotional life of
the Romantic poets, and received by way of artistic
inheritance a temperament already sensitive to a
thousand influences that would have left the men
of an earlier century unmoved; and to these inherited aptitudes for feeling subtly and richly were
added all the half-tones and minor gradations of
feeling that the intense spiritual and intellectual
life of the post-Romantic period tended to develop.
With this exquisitely sensitive temperament, he
looked on the outside world and found everywhere
correspondences between his moods and the aspects
of nature. To catch and interpret, in all its range
and subtlety and evanescent beauty, this emotional
suggestiveness of nature was Tennyson's task, just
as Wordsworth's task was to catch and register
its moral and spiritual suggestiveness. Tennyson's
poetry, then, may be regarded as in a very special
sense, a continuation of the Wordsworthian tradition, and as carrying still further that subdual
of nature to the needs of man's spirit that Wordsworth wrought at so faithfully.

The variety and the subtlety of Tennyson's
moods are most noticeable when we turn from his
treatment of landscape to his use of natural sights
and sounds as symbols. It is, of course, only by

the use of these symbols that he could hope to suggest the thousand and one changes of mood he tried
to portray.   These evanescent moods have no
names; there are no conventional signs that the poet
can use to place them before his readers; hence for
each mood he must find some natural equivalent —
some symbol that shall stand in its place, and, by
touching secret springs in our minds and hearts,
evoke the subtle complex of feeling he aims to suggest. These equivalents and symbols Tennyson
finds chiefly in nature; and his use of them is the
last means to be noted by which he brings about a
closer union between matter and spirit.

This symbolical use of nature, together with its
effect in giving a spiritual meaning to the world of
the senses, is well illustrated in the lyric, "Tears,
idle tears." The mood that the thought of the past
calls up is highly complex — a resultant of many
strangely blending elements; and the poet uses a
series of sensuous images, a series of natural sights
and sounds, to suggest the elementary feelings that
enter into this mood. The "freshness" of delight
with which the past is for a moment restored,
the infinite "sadness" with which its irrevocable-
ness forces itself once more on the thought, the
"strangeness" of the far-away dim regions of
memory, — these are the notes of feeling that go to
make up the whole rich chord of the mood; and
each has as its symbol, to call it into being, an
image from nature : —

" Fresh as the first beam glittering on a sail,
    That brings our friends up from the under-world,
    Sad as the last which reddens over one
    That sinks with all we love below the verge ;
    So sad, so fresh, the days that are no more.

" Ah, sad and strange as in dark summer dawns
    The earliest pipe of half-awaken'd birds
    To dying ears, when unto dying eyes
    The casement slowly grows a glimmering square ;
    So sad, so strange, the days that are no more."

Each of the images in these verses is a symbol
charged with feeling.   And not only does the series
of symbols serve to suggest at the moment of reading the precise mood of the poet, but always there-
after a reddening sail at sunset and the song of
birds at dawn mean something more to us than
they meant before Tennyson used them as symbols.
Nature has taken on a whole new range of spiritual
associations.

There are later poets who have surpassed Tennyson in variety and complexity of mood and in suggestiveness and subtlety of symbolic phrasing.   In
both these respects Dante Gabriel Rossetti was
probably Tennyson's superior.   But his superiority
was gained at great cost.   Nature, in his poetry, is
broken up into a mere collection of symbolic sights
and sounds ; we miss the breadth of treatment and
the fine open-air quality of Tennyson's work ; there
is often a sense of artificiality, of exaggeration,
almost of violence done to nature to force her into
the service of the poet's moods.   Moreover, the

variety and the subtlety of Rossetti's moods are
gained at a like cost. Delight in moods became
with Rossetti moodiness, and the study of moods
reached the point of morbid introspection: subjectivity became a disease.

Tennyson, then, resembles the Romantic poets in
his lack of sympathy with real life. He lived in a
dream-world rather than in the world of real men
and real women; and it is this dream-world, with
its iridescence of beauty and its simplified and
intensified characters, that he portrays for us in his
poetry, save where he shows us the distorted pictures of life to be found in the minds of men half-
mad with disappointed passion. His impatience of
conventional life, his lack of interest in concrete
character, and his intense subjectivity mark him
out as akin to the Romantic poets, and as not
having passed so decisively beyond the Romantic
point of view and the Romantic mood as Browning,
for example, passed beyond them. He was like
the Romantic poets, too, in the fact that it was
to nature that he turned to find escape from the
crude actualities of everyday life; and it is probably through his share in the great Romantic work
of spiritualizing nature that he will be most en-
duringly influential.

HAWTHORNE

It used to be the fashion a generation ago to
have much to say about the morbidness of the life
that Hawthorne's stories portray. But of late
years the decadents have been in their romances so
ingeniously busy with disease and death that to
turn back to Hawthorne seems like returning to
nature — to what is normal and healthy and sana-
tive. It may, indeed, be true that Hawthorne had
a hypertrophied conscience, and that the portrayal
of life seemed to him chiefly worth while because
it gave him a chance to indulge that conscience in
its somewhat morbid desire to be troublesome.
But, after all, to have an overanxious conscience is
a more human state of affairs than to have, as is so
often true of the decadents, no conscience at all, or
to have one only to the end that clever defiance of
it may lead to finely calculated discords in the
music of art. Just here lies the difference between
the novels of Hawthorne and the stories that modern decadence is so liberal with. In both forms of
art, sin, disease, death, the grisliest facts of human
destiny are perpetually in evidence; but Hawthorne is sincere in dealing with them, and meas-

ures their results and computes their meaning in
terms of normal life and the conventional moral
consciousness, whereas modern decadents are primarily concerned to juggle out of the evil facts of
life and their impact on our moral nature some
new fantastic artistic effect, and care not a doit for
the ethical point of view.

It is amusing to find Hawthorne now and then
having an inkling of the existence of the primrose
path of decadence, or coquetting with the notion of
irresponsibility. In the *Blithedale Romance* he
seems nearest to defying his conscience and being
recklessly studious of artistic effects for their own
dear sakes. Miles Coverdale, who tells the story,
is, as he assures us, "a devoted epicure of his own
emotions." In one place, after describing a mood
in which "the actual world" was robbed for him
"of its solidity," Coverdale tells us, in a self-satis-
fied way, that he "resolved to pause and enjoy the
moral sillabub" of the mood "until it was quite
dissolved away." In another place he confesses to
the habit of observing and analyzing from a distance the characters of his fellows, and he is evi-
dently somewhat proud of his speculative and half-
cynical detachment. "It is not, I apprehend, a
healthy kind of mental occupation," he declares,
with apparently a pleasant sense of abnormality,
"to devote one's self too exclusively to the study
of individual men and women." Yet despite a few
such superficial symptoms of dilettantism, Coverdale

has a very respectable conscience, which insinuates its vigorous prejudices into his interpretation of the lives and actions he is observing and reporting.

What is true of Coverdale is true in a yet higher degree of Hawthorne's other characters; sooner or later they all become acutely aware of having fostered or violated a Puritan conscience — with the possible exception of Zenobia; and on her, poor woman! Hawthorne, while he portrays her, keeps fixed a kind of evil eye, which ultimately drives her into suicide as the only fitting expiation for her venturesome originality. As for Donatello, in the *Marble Faun*, who is at the start ostensibly the very type of unmoral humanity, he is, despite all his flourish of animality, never anything else than a thoroughly well-tamed creature, fit to caper in a lady's chamber. His wildness is a hothouse wildness, a studio wildness, a manipulated, carefully fostered wildness, that is useful only for purposes of ornament and demonstration. When one really contemplates Donatello in the light of modern science, there is something curiously grotesque in trying to regard Hawthorne's Faun as the Missing Link or as Primeval Man before he evolved a conscience. There is more of outdoors in one verse of Walt Whitman's than in all Hawthorne's pages about Donatello.

No; the simple truth is that Hawthorne is in all his romances normal in spite of himself, and persistently moral and ethical in his interests despite

his constitutional unsociability, his contempt for
conventions, and his overweening imaginativeness.
He is ruled by his Puritan ancestors, and in his
most fantastic individual dreams is loyal to inherited moral prejudices. His earnestness of purpose
and his unfailing moral scrupulousness give to his
dream-world and its shadowy populace a genuine-
ness and cogency which the art of the decadents,
dealing as it does in many of the same *motifs*,
never rivals.

Still, it remains true that not more with Hawthorne than with the decadents are we in the
actual world of every day. Hawthorne is a
dreamer who "dreams *true*," but who, nevertheless,
merely *dreams*, and whose world has the delicate
intangibility of all dream-worlds. We never
escape, in reading Hawthorne's romances, from the
temperament of the author, and from his unobtru-
sive but persistent imaginative control. He
creates for a purpose, and in each romance he subdues to this purpose the background, the incident,
the plot, the characters, and even the imagery and
phrasing. The thoroughness with which his generating purpose runs through every detail and word
of a romance, and fashions and tempers and unifies
all to a single predetermined end, is one of the
most convincing proofs of Hawthorne's power as
an imaginative artist. There is no piecemeal
working in Hawthorne — none of the haphazard
procedure that takes details and suggestions good-

naturedly as chance offers them and weaves them dextrously, as Thackeray, for example, is wont to do, into a motley web of fiction. Each of Hawthorne's long romances is a perfectly wrought work of art, wherein every part is nicely aware of all the rest and of the central purpose and total effect.

Hawthorne is a master spinner of beautiful webs, and the most rabid devotee of art for art's sake cannot well refuse to enjoy the fineness and consistency of his designs, the continuity and firmness of his texture, and the richness and depth of his tinting. The pattern, to be sure, always contains a moral for apt pupils. But though Hawthorne dreams in terms of the ten commandments, he dreams beauty none the less; and, indeed, for some of us who still believe that life is greater than art, his dreams are all the more fascinating artistically because they are deeply, darkly, beautifully true. Dreaming, that in all its wayward caprice is delicately aware of the worth of the moral law and the rational bias at the heart of things, and pays a pretty respect to the categorical imperative and the principle of sufficient reason, seems after all to gain an intensity and force and persuasive beauty not otherwise to be won.

In all his romances Hawthorne is more or less plainly in pursuit of some moral or spiritual truth. In the desire to illustrate such a truth is to be found the originating motive of each of his longer works. The *Scarlet Letter* is the Romance of Expi-

ation, done in deeply glowing colours against the
dark, sullen background of the Puritan temperament. *The House of the Seven Gables* is the Romance of Heredity. The colours are gray and
sombre, with some pretty fantastic detail in pale
rose and green where Phœbe's tender girlishness or
womanliness appears. The *Marble Faun* is the
Romance of the Mystery of Evil. It is the most
elaborate of all Hawthorne's stories, and as a work
of art is nearer lacking unity of tone and design,
because of the archæological and landscape detail
of which the author is so lavish. Yet even here
the background, though elaborate, has propriety.
The story deals in symbolic form with the deepest
mystery of human destiny — the origin and the
meaning of evil; and the background for the action
is Rome, the very stones of whose streets tell tales
of the struggles toward good and toward evil of
many races of men. Rome, with its long perspec-
tives through a picturesque past, is the symbol of
civilized man in all his history, from the far away
origin of society down to latter-day love of anarchy.
Against this background is depicted the symbolic
fate of Donatello and Hilda and Miriam, as types
of the human will in its relation to evil.

For the analyst of novelists' methods there is a
real delight to be won from noting how consistent
Hawthorne is in constructing his stories. He
works invariably just as he ought to work to suit
the theorist's notions. Being a creator of allegor-

H

ical romances, he ought to work from within his
own mind out toward the world of actual fact, for
which world he should have a fine disdain.　His
main purpose should be the creation and illustration of moral effects.　In an essay on Hawthorne's
Tales, Poe has very happily laid down the law for
this kind of fiction: "A skilful literary artist has
constructed a tale.　If wise, he has not fashioned
his thoughts to accommodate his incidents, but
having conceived, with deliberate care, a certain
unique or single *effect* to be wrought out, he then
invents such incidents — he then combines such
events — as may best aid him in establishing this
preconceived effect.　If his very initial sentence
tend not to the outbringing of this effect, then he
has failed in his first step.　In the whole composi-
tion there should be no word written of which the
tendency, direct or indirect, is not to the one pre-
established design."　All these prescriptions,
which, according to Poe, should govern the short
tale, will be found duly observed in Hawthorne's
long romances.　In tale and romance Hawthorne's
methods are nearly the same.　His imagination, in
its dreamy play over the records of the remote
drama of life, has been fascinated by some one of
its typical and oft-recurring aspects — the bitterness of the expiation of sin, the tragic oppression
wherewith the vices and even the virtues of the
past weigh down on the innocent present.　Such a
large aspect of life usually carries with it into the

dark-chamber of Hawthorne's mind some typical
man or woman whose character and fate incarnate
for him, with picturesque detail, the special truths
about life that for the time being preoccupy him.
From these original elements, the action of the
story and all subordinate detail gradually shape
themselves forth and take shadowy form, never
with the wish or the hope of bringing the reader
close to some glaring piece of actual life, but
always with the aim of enveloping him subduingly
in an atmosphere of spiritual emotion, and of offering him unobtrusively at every moment, in the acts,
in the thoughts and feelings of the actors, in the
byways and vistas of nature, in the very air that
he breathes, hints and symbols of certain large
truths about human life and human endeavour.
The regions where the action takes place are oftenest nameless; they are in dreamland — "vaporous,
unaccountable, forlorn of light;" they are not veri-
fiable as actual corners of the world-ball, unless
they are already so instinct with romance as to be
fit to conspire with the author's purpose and help
on the moral necromancy. The people that inhabit
this dream-world are "goblins of flesh and blood";
they are spirited up before us out of an unknown
past. Priscilla, Hawthorne assures us, seemed to
have "fallen out of the clouds"; Miriam's past
and even large parts of her present are tantalizingly unverifiable. The gossip of those who sur-
round the principal actors tends to veil them still

more deftly in a dim cloud of strangeness, rather than to expound their personalities with scientific accuracy, as would happen in a modern realistic story. We never know thoroughly the details of the lives of Chillingworth or Donatello; we are kept in uncertainty about them through surmises and suspicions that run in the story from lip to lip. What is sure about such characters is their pursuit of a few symbolic purposes which serve to fit them unerringly into the large design of the fable. Donatello is all the time busied with the process of getting a soul. Judge Pyncheon is bent on selfish triumph at all costs, in pursuit of hereditary schemes of aggrandizement. Dimmesdale writhes his way pallidly through the *Scarlet Letter*, — hand on heart, — the visible symbol of repentance. Neither in these characters nor in any others is there an attempt at thoroughness or minuteness of realization, or at any delicate complication of motives or at scientific analysis. Hawthorne keeps his characterization carefully free from the intricacies of actual life, and preserves uncontaminate the large outlines and glowing colours of his simplified men and women. Even in speech the people of his stories are nicely unreal; his workmen are choice in their English, and his children lisp out sentences that are prettily modelled. Here, as so often, Hawthorne cares nothing for crude fact.

His world, too, is a world where symbols are as frequent as in the happy days before Newton, the

arch-foe of symbols, unwove the rainbow. The
main action itself of each romance is one great
symbol, and it germinates persistently in minor
symbols. Scarlet letters flash out unexpectedly,
even on the face of the heavens; the House of the
Seven Gables visibly shadows Hepzibah, Clifford,
and Phœbe with the evil influences of the past;
Hilda's doves encircle her and her tower with suggestions of unsullied innocence. So, too, Hawthorne's characters themselves have features or
tricks of manner that mark them out as symbolic
and as meaning more than meets the eye; Donatello's ears, Priscilla's tremulous, listening look,
Dimmesdale's persistent clutching at his heart,
tease the reader into a continuous sense of the
haunted duplicity of the world in which Hawthorne keeps him. In each of Hawthorne's romances the world and its inhabitants echo and re-
echo a single importunate thought.

Of course, all this is very sadly removed from
the kind of art that the realists of recent years
have instructed us to delight in. No one of literary experience can cheat himself into fancying
as he reads Hawthorne that he is having to do
with real men or women or treading the solid
ground of fact. He is continually aware that the
world he moves in has been tampered with. Nevertheless, Hawthorne's fiction is bound to remain
for most readers — both for uncritical readers and
for readers of cultivation and discernment, even

for those of them who are completely familiar
with the best work of the modern realists — a permanent source of delight. And this is true for
various reasons. The lover of skilful technique,
whatever his theory of the ultimate aims of fiction,
must relish the beauty of Hawthorne's workman-
ship. No one can gainsay Hawthorne's skill of
execution, the largeness and symmetry of his designs, his delicately sure manipulation of detail,
the intelligence of his methods when his ends are
once granted, the freedom and uninterruptedness
of his draughting, and the perfect graduation of
his tones. Then, too, his romances have an
abiding source of charm, whatever the fluctuations
of fashion, in the fineness and nobleness of the temperament in terms of which they make life over.
Doubtless this temperament has its limitations.
Hawthorne's conscience was a familiar spirit that
would not be laid, and Hawthorne allowed himself
to be driven to the almost invariable study of path-
ological states of soul and the analysis of guilt and
expiation, until a reader is tempted to exclaim that
life for Hawthorne is seven-eighths conduct and
the other eighth remorse. Still, through all this inherited Puritanic gloom there runs continually an
unsubduable love for human nature, which makes
the world of Hawthorne's stories a hospitable
region, and gives the reader a sense of well-being
even in the midst of the misdeeds and repentances
through which he makes his way. He feels that

he breathes a genuine atmosphere of human sympathy; tenderness and love, all the elemental affections that form the abidingly worthy substance of human nature, are generously active in Hawthorne's men and women — his people are real enough for that; and, moreover, Hawthorne, the author, bears himself toward all the folk of his mimic drama with large-hearted charity and indefatigable faith in the essential rightness of the universe. The romances are, to quote Hawthorne's own words, "true to the human heart," and the human heart, as Hawthorne interprets it, is a very lovable and love-disseminating organ. For their rich, strong humanity, Hawthorne's romances will long be gratefully read by all who either naïvely or instructedly believe life to be worth living.

Sometimes one is tempted to regret that Hawthorne did not oftener forego his artificial atmospheres and his elaborate symbolism, and deal sincerely and directly with the actual life of his day and generation. Poe urged this on Hawthorne, and took him roundly to task for following so inveterately the *high priori*, allegorical way. In point of fact, Hawthorne has, in one or two of his *Twice Told Tales*, actually reproduced bits of the New England life that surrounded him — for example, in the sketch called the *Apple-Dealer*. Moreover, he has portrayed very truly and delightfully, in the Introduction to the *Scarlet Letter*, the precincts of the quaint custom-house of Salem, with its retinue of lackadaisical, sleepy officials. Yet it is to be noted that these subjects from actual life which he has treated sympathetically and convincingly are all of the sort where life in its monotony and patience of trifles and dimness of detail almost passes over into the region of dreams. It may be doubted whether a more variegated life and more complex and brilliant characters would not have been beyond Hawthorne's power of truthful representation. He had in very fact something of the night in his disposition, and whatever he prevailingly portrays has either to have in its nature a suggestion of the discoloured temperateness of night, or else to be thinned away and modulated through his imagination until it has lost the grossness and actuality of fact and grown tenuous and pallid.

In his *causeries*, where he professes to talk to the reader directly about the commonplace affairs of daily life, there is noticeable the same reduction of all things to the texture of a dream, the same disenthralment of the most prosaic objects and facts from the tyranny of material law and everyday aspect. We can fancy Hawthorne writing the weird tale of a man who found whatever he touched melt into an impalpable dream, and who was thus doomed to wander ever in a region of enchanted, intangible forms. This man may typify Hawthorne himself; only it must be noted that his dream-world has stability and truth and a welcome

for us because of its faithfulness to the great laws
of human nature, to the moral law, to the best feelings of good men and good women, and also because of its exquisite consistency and the beauty of
its fluent self-revelation. We dream uninterrupt-
edly in accordance with certain essential needs of
our natures, and we instinctively accept the dream
without any jarring desire to compare it with
crude fact.

What oftenest disturbs the modern and exacting
reader of Hawthorne, and rouses him unpleasantly
from his dream, is Hawthorne's abuse of symbols.
Now and then, Hawthorne's instinct fails him in
making the nice distinction between art and artifice. In his creation of atmosphere and search for
effect he is occasionally obvious and cheap, and
seems to tamper needlessly with facts and with the
laws of nature. The heat of the scarlet letter becomes after a time oppressive; the display of the
A in the heavens, during the scene on the scaffold,
seems merely a theatrical bid for a shiver. The
shadow that is asserted always to have rested on
Chillingworth, even in the sunshine, seems the
result of a gratuitous juggling with the laws of
light. Now and again, in such cases as these, Hawthorne makes us aware that he is playing tricks on
our souls. Matthew Arnold has quoted Sainte-
Beuve as somewhere saying that every kind of art
has its characteristic defect, and that the defect of
Romantic art is *le faux*. From this falseness

Hawthorne keeps, on the whole, wonderfully free; and yet at times he is betrayed into it.

Ordinarily, with Romantic writers, artificiality comes from the exaggerated study of an effect that is purely artistic; but with Hawthorne this is not so. His desire to point his moral is what misleads him — his monomaniac wish to find the heavens and the earth eloquent of the special truth that for the moment rules his imagination. This wish in one form or another pervades, as we have seen, all Hawthorne's fiction; and as long as it acts silently and unobtrusively, like gravity or the law of chemical affinities, to bind Hawthorne's world harmoniously together and to make it a significant whole, its presence is not only unobjectionable, but is largely responsible for the cogency and impressiveness of his art. But when this underlying moral impulse plays symbolic tricks with trifles, it degenerates from being a natural power into a kind of cheap legerdemain, and becomes little short of offensive. At such moments Hawthorne's absorbing preoccupation with a moral meaning and unstudiousness of artistic effect, pure and simple, seem almost ludicrous to a modern reader who has been trained to delight in the skill with which sophisticated artists nowadays vanquish technical difficulties for their own sake and embody a mood or realize a situation with single-minded pleasure in their art and without moral malice prepense. At times, then, Hawthorne must impress us as naïve in his devotion

to fairly obvious moral truth ; and at times, too, he
seems naïve in his ambitions. It would require
great courage for any one nowadays to attempt to
solve in a romance the mystery of the existence of
evil. Occasionally, Hawthorne is naïve in his
enthusiasms, particularly in the *Marble Faun.* The
descriptions of Rome and its works of art have something of the exuberance of the first tour in Europe.
The praise of Guido woos nowadays unsympathetic
ears, and in general the discussions on art that the
American colony in the *Marble Faun* solemnly en-
gage in are quite sufficiently obvious and archaic.

Finally, it must be admitted that Hawthorne has
never studied or portrayed sympathetically a man
or woman of real intellectual quality ; he has never
put before us a first-rate mind in perfect working
order, nor anywhere traced out, subtly and convincingly, the refinements of the intellectual life. It
is not simply that he has never given us a genuine
man of the world ; of course, his method and temperament alike forbade that. From the very nature
of Hawthorne's art, a man of the world, had Hawthorne tried to portray him, would have become a
man out of the world. But why should not Hawthorne have portrayed, at least once in a way, a
thoroughly intellectual man or woman ? a man or
woman whose mind was well disciplined, brilliant,
and controlling ? Nowhere has he done this. His
men, the moment they grow accomplished, drift
into morbidness or villainy — hunt the philoso-

pher's stone, become grotesque philanthropists, take to mesmerism or alchemy or unwise experiments in matrimony. Hawthorne's fiction seems really somewhat vitiated by Romantic distrust of scholarship, of mental acuteness, and of whatever savours of the pride of intellect. This bias in his nature must be borne in mind when one is considering the shallowness and defectiveness of the individual characterization in his novels — a shallowness and defectiveness which, as has been noted, are involved in his essentially romantic conception of the art of fiction.

Yet, when all these disturbing elements in our enjoyment of Hawthorne have been allowed for, there remains a vast fund of often almost unalloyed delight to be won from his writings. Moreover, this delight seems likely to increase rather than grow less. At present, Hawthorne is at a decided disadvantage, because, while remote enough to seem in trifles here and there archaic, he is yet not remote enough to escape contemporary standards or to be read with imaginative historical allowances and sympathy, as Richardson or Defoe is read. Hawthorne's romances have the human quality and the artistic beauty that ensure survival; and in a generation or two, when the limitations of the Romantic ideal and the scope of Romantic methods have become historically clear in all men's minds, Hawthorne's novels will be read with an even surer sense than exists to-day of that beauty

of form and style and that tender humanity which
come from the individuality of their author, and
with a more tolerant comprehension of the imper-
fectness of equipment and occasional faults of manner that were the result of his environment and
age.

EDGAR ALLAN POE

POE is a better poet in his prose than in his poetry. A reader of Poe's poetry, if he be quick to take umbrage at artificiality and prone to cavil, feels, after a dozen poems, like attempting an inventory of Poe's literary workshop — the material Poe uses is so uniform and the objects he fashions are so few and inevitable. The inventory might run somewhat as follows: One plaster bust of Pallas slightly soiled; one many-wintered Raven croaking *Nevermore;* a parcel of decorative names — Auber, Yaanek, Zante, Israfel; a few robes of sorrow, a somewhat frayed funeral pall, and a coil of Conqueror Worms; finally, one beautiful lay figure whom the angels name indifferently Lenore, Ulalume, and Annabel Lee. Masterly as is Poe's use of this poetical outfit, subtle as are his cadences and his sequences of tone-colour, it is only rarely that he makes us forget the cleverness of his manipulation and wins us into accepting his moods and imagery with that unconscious and almost hypnotic subjection to his will which the true poet secures from his readers.

In the best of his visionary *Tales*, on the other
hand, Poe is much more apt to have his way with
us. He works with a far greater variety of appli-
ances, which it is by no means easy to number and
call by name; the effects he aims at are manifold
and not readily noted and classified; and the details that his imagination elaborates come upon us
with a tropical richness and apparent confusion
that mimic well the splendid lawlessness and un-
designedness of nature. Moreover, even if the
artifice in these tales were more palpable than it
is, it would be less offensive than in poetry, in-
asmuch as the standard of sincerity is in such per-
formances confessedly less exacting. The likeness
in aim and in effect between the tales and the
poems, however, cannot be missed — between such
tales as *Ligeia* and *Eleonora* and such poems as
The Raven and *Ulalume*. Mr. Leslie Stephen has
somewhere spoken of De Quincey's impassioned
prose as aiming to secure in unmeasured speech
very many of the same effects that Keats's *Odes*
produce in authentic verse. This holds true also
of the best of Poe's romances; they are really
prose-poems. And, indeed, Poe has himself recognized in his essay on Hawthorne the close kinship
between tale and poem, assigning to the poem subjects in the treatment of which the creation of
beauty is the ruling motive, and leaving to the
prose tale the creation of all other single effects,
such as horror, humour, and terror. Both poem and

tale must be brief, absolutely unified, and must create a single overwhelming mood.

The world that Poe's genuinely fantastic tales take us into has the burnish, the glow, the visionary radiance of the world of Romantic poetry; it is as luxuriantly unreal, too, as phantasmagoric — though it lacks the palpitating, buoyant loveliness of the nature that such poets as Shelley reveal, and is somewhat enamelled or metallic in its finish. Its glow and burnish come largely from the concreteness of Poe's imagination, from his inveterate fondness for sensations, for colour, for light, for luxuriant vividness of detail. Poe had the tingling senses of the genuine poet, senses that vibrated like delicate silver wire to every impact. He was an amateur of sensations and loved to lose himself in the *O Altitudo* of a perfume or a musical note. He pored over his sensations and refined upon them, and felt to the core of his heart the peculiar thrill that darted from each. He had seventy times seven colours in his emotional rainbow, and was swift to fancy the evanescent hue of feeling that might spring from every sight or sound — from the brazen note, for example, of the clock in *The Masque of the Red Death*, from "the slender stems" of the ebony and silver trees in *Eleonora*, or from the "large and luminous orbs" of Ligeia's eyes. Out of the vast mass of these vivid sensations — "passion-wingèd ministers of thought" — Poe shaped and fashioned the world in which his romances confine us, a world that is, therefore, scintillating and burnished and vibrant, quite unlike the world in Hawthorne's tales, which is woven out of dusk and moonlight.

Yet, curiously enough, this intense brilliancy of surface does not tend to exorcise mystery, strangeness, terror from Poe's world, or to transfer his stories into the region of everyday fact. Poe is a conjurer who does not need to have the lights turned down. The effects that he is most prone to aim at are, of course, the shivers of awe, crispings of the nerves, shuddering thrills that come from a sudden, overwhelming sense of something uncanny, abnormal, ghastly, lurking in the heart of life. And these nervous perturbations are even more powerfully excited by those of his stories that, like *Eleonora* and *Ligeia*, have a lustrous finish, than by sketches that, like *Shadow and Silence*, deal with twilight lands and half-visualized regions. In *The Masque of the Red Death*, in *The Fall of the House of Usher*, and in *A Descent into the Maelström*, the details of incident and background flash themselves on our imaginations with almost painful distinctness.

The terror in Poe's tales is not the terror of the child that cannot see in the dark, but the terror of diseased nerves and morbid imaginations, that see with dreadful visionary vividness and feel a mortal pang. Poe is a past master of the moods of diseased mental life, and in the interests of some one

I

or other of these semi-hysterical moods many of
his most uncannily prevailing romances are written.
They are prose-poems that realize for us such half-
frenetic glimpses of the world as madmen have;
and *suggest* in us for the moment the breathless,
haggard mood of the victim of hallucinations.

It must not, however, be forgotten that Poe wrote
tales of ratiocination as well as romances of death.
In his ability to turn out with equal skill stories
bordering on madness and stories where intellectual analysis, shrewd induction, reasoning upon
evidence, all the processes of typically sane mental
life, are carried to the utmost pitch of precision
and effectiveness, lies one of the apparent anomalies
of Poe's genius and art.   In *The Murders in the
Rue Morgue, The Mystery of Marie Rogêt,* and *The
Purloined Letter,* Poe seems sanity incarnate, pure
mental energy untouched by moods or passions,
weaving and unweaving syllogisms and tracking out
acutely the subtlest play of thought.   What in
these stories has become of Poe the fancy-monger,
the mimic maniac, the specialist in moodiness and
abnormality ?

After all, the difficulty here suggested is only
superficial and yields speedily to a little careful
analysis.   We have not really to deal with a puzzling case of double personality, with an author
who at his pleasure plays at being Dr. Jekyll or
Mr. Hyde.   In all Poe's stories the same personality
is at work, the same methods are followed, and the

material used, though at first sight it may seem in
the two classes of tales widely diverse, will also
turn out to be quite the same, at any rate in its
artificiality, in its remoteness from real complex
human nature, and in its origin in the mind of the
author. Certain instructions that in an essay on
Hawthorne Poe has given to would-be writers of
tales are delightfully serviceable to the anxious
unraveller of the apparent contradictions in Poe's
personality.

To him who would fashion a successful short
story, Poe prescribes as follows: He must first of
all pick out an effect — it may be of horror, it may
be of humour, it may be of terror — which his short
story is to aim to produce, to impose vibratingly
on the temperament of its readers. This effect is
to give the law to the whole of the short story, to
regulate its every detail, both of incident and character, its background of nature or town, its texture
of sensations, its imagery, phrasing, wording, tone,
even the cadences of its sentences. The very first
sentence must in some divining fashion prepare
for this effect, and every bit of material that is
used must help in the preparation, must be premonitory, must whet curiosity, must set the nerves
nicely a-tremble, must make the reader more and
more ready to fall a prey to the final catastrophe.
In short, the tale, as Poe conceives it, is a marvel-
lously ingenious set of devices for so tuning a sensitive temperament and giving it intensity of *timbre*

that at just the right moment a special chord of
music may be struck upon it with overwhelming
power and richness of overtone and resonance.
This formula applies alike to Poe's romances of
death and to his tales of ratiocination; and one
of the first suggestions it carries with it has to do
with the artificiality of the material that Poe uses
in all his fiction. Whether the effect that Poe
aims at is a shiver of surprise at the sudden ingenious resolution of a riddle, or a shudder of horror
at the collapse of a haunted house, his methods of
work are substantially the same, and the stuff from
which he weaves his tale is equally unreal and remote from what ordinary life has to offer; it is all
the product of an infinitely inventive intellect that
devises and plans and adroitly arranges with an
unflinching purpose to attain an effect. The better
poetry, the more feigning; and Poe is an excellent
poet in these prose-poems. He can invent with
endless ingenuity and plausibility, play-passions,
play-moods, play-sensations, play-ideas, and play-
complications of incident. He is an adept in fitting
these mock images of life deftly together, in subtly
arranging these simulacra of real feeling and real
thought so that they shall have complete congruity, shall have the glamour and the momentary
plausibility of truth, and shall rally together at
the right moment in a perfect acclaim of music.
But whether the tale deal professedly with abnormal life or with rational life, its seemliness and

beauty and persuasive power come simply from
Poe's immense cleverness as a constructive artist,
as a technician, from his ability to play tunes on
temperaments, not from his honest command of
human life and character.   In all that he does Poe
is emotionally shallow but artistically, like Joey
Bagstock, "devilish sly."

The shallowness of Poe's treatment of life and
character is almost too obvious to need illustration.
Not only does he disdain, as Hawthorne disdains,
to treat any individual character with minute realistic detail, but he does not even portray typical
characters in their large outlines, with a view to
opening before us the permanent springs of human
action or putting convincingly before us the radical elements of human nature.   The actors in his
stories are all one-idea'd creatures, monomaniac
victims of passion, or grief, or of some perverse
instinct, or of an insane desire to guess riddles.
They are magniloquent *poseurs*, who dine off their
hearts in public, or else morbidly ingenious in-
tellects for the solving of complicated problems.
The worthy Nietzsche declares somewhere that the
actors in Wagner's music-dramas are always just a
dozen steps from the mad-house.   We may say the
same of Poe's characters, with the exception of
those that are merely Babbage calculating ma-
chines.   Complex human characters, characters
that are approximately true to the whole range
of human motive and interest, Poe never gives

us. He conceives of characters merely as means for securing his artificial effects on the nerves of his readers.

The world, too, into which Poe takes us, burnished as it is, vividly visualized as it is, is a counterfeit world, magnificently false like his characters. Sometimes it is a phantasmagoric world, full of romantic detail and sensuous splendour. Its bright meadows are luxuriant with asphodels, hyacinths, and acanthuses, are watered with limpid rivers of silence that lose themselves shimmeringly in blue Da Vinci distances, are lighted by triple-tinted suns, and are finally shut in by the "golden walls of the universe." When not an exotic region of this sort, Poe's world is apt to be a dextrously contrived toy universe, full of trap-doors, unexpected passages, and clever mechanical devices of all sorts, fit to help the conjurer in securing his effects. Elaborately artificial in some fashion or other, Poe's world is sure to be, designed with nice malice to control the reader's imagination and put it at Poe's mercy. In short, in all that he does, in the material that he uses, in the characters that he conjures up to carry on the action of his stories, in his methods of weaving together incident and description and situation and action, Poe is radically artificial, a calculator of effects, a reckless scorner of fact and of literal truth.

And, indeed, it is just this successful artificiality that for many very modern temperaments consti-

tutes Poe's special charm; he is thoroughly irresponsible; he whistles the commonplace down the
wind and forgets everything but his dream, its
harmony, its strenuous flight, its splendour and
power. The devotees of art for art's sake have
now for many years kept up a tradition of un-
stinted admiration for Poe. This has been specially true in France, where, indeed, men of all
schools have joined in doing him honour. Barbey
d'Aurevilly wrote an eulogistic essay on him as
early as 1853, an essay to which he has since from
time to time made various additions, the last in
1883. Baudelaire translated Poe's tales in several
instalments between 1855 and 1865. Émile Hennequin published, a few years ago, an elaborate
study and life of Poe; and Stéphane Mallarmé has
of late conferred a new and perhaps somewhat dubious immortality upon the *Raven*, through a translation into very symbolistic prose. In truth, Poe
was a decadent before the days of decadence, and
he has the distinction of having been one of the
earliest defiant practisers of art for art's sake.
In his essay on the *Poetic Principle*, he expressly
declared that a poem should be written solely "for
the poem's sake," — a phrase which almost antici-
pates the famous formula of modern æstheticism.
The drift of this essay, Poe's opinion elsewhere
recorded, and his practice as a story-teller, all agree
in implying or urging that art is its own justifica-
tion, that the sole aim of art is the creation of

beauty, and that art and actual life need have nothing to do with one another. To be sure, Poe's comments on everyday life have not acquired quite the exquisite contempt and the epigrammatic finish characteristic of modern decadence; yet the root of the matter was in Poe — witness a letter in which he boasts of his insensibility to the charms of "temporal life," and of being "profoundly excited" solely "by music and by some poems."

Poe and his heroes curiously anticipate, in many respects, the morbid dreamers whom French novelists of the decadent school have of recent years repeatedly studied, and of whom Huysmans's Des Esseintes may be taken as a type. The hero in *The Fall of the House of Usher*, with his "cadaverousness of complexion," his "eye large, liquid, and luminous beyond comparison," his "habitual trepidancy," his "hollow-sounding enunciation," "his morbid acuteness of the senses," and his suffering when exposed to the odours of certain flowers and to all sounds save those of a few stringed instruments, might be a preliminary study for Huysmans's memorable Des Esseintes. Usher has not the French hero's sophistication and self-consciousness; he suffers dumbly, and has not Des Esseintes's consolation in knowing himself a "special soul," supersensitive and delicate beyond the trite experience of nerves and senses prescribed by practical life. He does not carry on his morbid experimentations debonairly as does Des Esseintes, and he takes his

diseases too seriously. But he nevertheless antici-
pates Des Esseintes astonishingly in looks, in nerves,
in physique, and even in tricks of manner. Poe's
heroes, too, are forerunners of modern decadents in
their refinings upon sensation, in their fusion of the
senses, and in their submergence in moods. As Herr
Nordau says of the Symbolists, they have eyes in
their ears; they see sounds; they smell colours.
One of them hears rays of light that fall upon his
retina. They are all extraordinarily alive to the
"unconsidered trifles" of sensation. The man in
the *Pit and the Pendulum* smells the odour of the
sharp steel blade that swings past him. They de-
tect with morbid delicacy of perception shades of
feeling that give likeness to the most apparently
diverse sensations. The lover in *Ligeia* feels in
his "intense scrutiny of Ligeia's eyes" the same
sentiment that at other times overmasters him "in
the survey of a rapidly growing vine, in the con-
templation of a moth, a butterfly, . . . in the falling of a meteor, . . . in the glances of unusually
aged people, . . ." and when listening to "certain
sounds from stringed instruments." Moods become
absorbing and monopolizing in the lives of these
vibrating temperaments. "Men have called me
mad," the lover in *Eleonora* ingratiatingly assures
us; "but the question is not yet settled whether
madness is or is not the loftiest intelligence;
whether much that is glorious, whether all that is
profound, does not spring from disease of thought

—from moods of mind exalted at the expense of the general intellect." Finally, Poe's heroes anticipate the heroes of modern decadence in feeling the delicate artistic challenge of sin and of evil: they hardly reach the audacities of French Diabolism and Sadism; but at least they have the whim of doing or fancying moral evil that æsthetic good may come.

All these characteristics of Poe's work may be summed up by saying that his heroes are apt to be neuropaths or degenerates. And doubtless Poe himself was a degenerate, if one cares to use the somewhat outworn idiom of the evangelist of the Philistines. He had the ego-mania of the degenerate, a fact which shows itself strikingly in his art through his preoccupation with death. In his poetry and prose alike the fear of death as numbing the precious core of personality is an obsession with him, and such subjects as premature burial, metempsychosis, revivification after death, the sensations that may go with the change from mortality to immortality (see the *Colloquy of Monos and Una*), had an irresistible fascination for him. Moreover, throughout Poe's art there are signs of ego-mania in the almost entire lack of the social sympathies. Where in Poe's stories do we find portrayed the sweet and tender relationships and affections that make human life endurable? Where are friendship and frank comradeship and the love of brothers and sisters and of parents and children? Where are

the somewhat trite but after all so necessary virtues
of loyalty, patriotism, courage, pity, charity, self-
sacrifice? Such old-fashioned qualities and ca-
pacities, the stuff out of which what is worth while
in human nature has heretofore been wrought,
are curiously unrecognized and unportrayed in
Poe's fiction. They seem to have had no artistic
meaning for him—these so obvious and commonplace elements in man and life. Perhaps they
simply seemed to him not the stuff that dreams are
made of.

When all is said, there is something a bit inhu-
man in Poe, which, while at times it may give a
special tinge to our pleasure in his art, occasionally
vitiates or destroys that pleasure. His taste is not
immaculate; he will go any length in search of a
shudder. Sometimes he is fairly repulsive because
of his callous recital of loathsome physical details,
for example in his description of the decimated
Brigadier-General, in *The Man that Was Used Up.*
In *King Pest, The Premature Burial,* and *M.
Valdemar,* there is this same almost vulgar insensibility in the presence of the unclean and dis-
gusting. At times, this callousness leads to artistic
mischance, and causes a shudder of laughter where
Poe wants a shiver of awe. Surely this is apt to
be the case in *Berenice,* the story where the hero
is fascinated by the beautiful teeth of the heroine,
turns amateur dentist after her death, and in a
frenzy of professional enthusiasm breaks open her

coffin, and extracts her incisors, bicuspids, and molars, thirty-two altogether — the set was complete.

When this inhumanity of Poe's does not lead to actual repulsiveness or to unintentional grotesqueness, it is nevertheless responsible for a certain aridity and intellectual cruelty that in the last analysis will be found pervading pretty much all he has written. This is what Barbey d'Aurevilly has in mind when he speaks of Poe's *sécheresse*, the terrible dryness of his art. And looking at the matter wholly apart from the question of ethics, this dryness is a most serious defect in Poe's work as an artist. His stories and characters have none of the buoyancy, the tender, elastic variableness, and the grace of living things; they are hard in finish, harsh in surface, mechanically inevitable in their working out. They seem calculated, the result of ingenious calculation, not because any particular detail impresses the reader as conspicuously false — Poe keeps his distance from life too skilfully and consistently for this — but because of their all-pervading lack of deeply human imagination and interest, because of that shallowness in Poe's hold upon life that has already been noted. The stories and the characters seem the work of pure intellect, of intellect divorced from heart; and for that very reason they do not wholly satisfy, when judged by the most exacting artistic standards. They seem the product of some ingenious mechanism for the manufacture of fiction, of some surpassing rival of Maelzel's chess-playing automaton. This faultily faultless accuracy and precision of movement may very likely be a penalty Poe has to submit to because of his devotion to art for art's sake. He is too much engrossed in treatment and manipulation; his dexterity of execution perhaps presupposes, at any rate goes along with, an almost exclusive interest in technical problems and in "effects," to the neglect of what is vital and human in the material he uses.

Closely akin to this dryness of treatment is a certain insincerity of tone or flourish of manner, that often interferes with our enjoyment of Poe. We become suddenly aware of the gleaming eye and complacent smile of the concealed manipulator in the writing-automaton. The author is too plainly lying in wait for us; or he is too ostentatiously exhibiting his cleverness and resource, his command of the tricks of the game. One of the worst things that can be said of Poe from this point of view is that he contains the promise and potency of Mr. Robert Hichens, and of other cheap English decadents. Poe himself is never quite a mere acrobat; but he suggests the possible coming of the acrobat, the clever tumbler with the ingenious grimace and the palm itching for coppers.

The same perfect mastery of technique that is characteristic of Poe's treatment of material is noticeable in his literary style. When one stops to consider it, Poe's style, particularly in his romances, is highly artificial, an exquisitely fabricated medium. Poe is fond of inversions and involutions in his sentence-structure, and of calculated rhythms that either throw into relief certain picturesque words, or symbolize in some reverberant fashion the mood of the moment. He seems to have felt very keenly the beauty of De Quincey's intricate and sophisticated cadences, and more than once he actually echoes some of the most noteworthy of them in his own distribution of accents. Special instances of this might be pointed out in *Eleonora* and in *The Premature Burial*. Poe's fondness for artificial musical effects is also seen in his emphatic reiteration of specially picturesque phrases, a trick of manner that every one associates with his poetry, and that is more than once found in his prose writings. "And, all at once, the moon arose through the thin ghastly mist, and was crimson in color. And mine eyes fell upon a huge gray rock which stood by the shore of the river, and was lighted by the light of the moon. And the rock was gray, and ghastly, and tall — and the rock was gray." Echolalia, Herr Nordau would probably call this trick in Poe's verse and prose, and he would regard it as an incontestable proof of Poe's degeneracy. Nevertheless, the beauty of the effects to which this mannerism leads in Poe's more artificial narratives is very marked.

In Poe's critical essays his style takes on an altogether different tone and movement, and becomes

analytical, rapid, incisive, almost acrid in its severity and intellectuality. The ornateness and the
beauty of cadence and colour that are characteristic
of his decorative prose disappear entirely. Significantly enough, Macaulay was his favourite literary
critic. "The style and general conduct of Macaulay's critical papers," Poe assures his readers,
"could scarcely be improved." A strange article
of faith to find in the literary creed of a dreamer,
an amateur of moods, an artistic epicure. Yet that
Poe was sincere in this opinion is proved by the
characteristics of his own literary essays. He
emulates Macaulay in his briskness, in the down-
rightness of his assertions, in his challengingly de-
monstrative tone, and in his unsensitiveness to the
artistic shade. Of course, he is far inferior to
Macaulay in knowledge and in thoroughness of
literary training, while he surpasses him in acuteness of analysis and in insight into technical
problems.

Poe's admiration for Macaulay and his emulation
of him in his critical writings are merely further
illustrations of the peculiar intellectual aridity that
has already been noted as characteristic of him.
Demonic intellectual ingenuity is almost the last
word for Poe's genius as far as regards his real
personality, the quintessential vital energy of the
man. His intellect was real; everything else about
him was exquisite feigning. His passion, his
human sympathy, his love of nature, all the emo-

tions that go into his fiction, have a counterfeit unreality about them. Not that they are actually hypocritical, but that they seem unsubstantial, mimetic, not the expression of a genuine nature. There was something of the cherub in Poe, and he had to extract his feelings from his head. Much of the time a reader of Poe is cajoled into a delighted forgetfulness of all this unreality, Poe is so adroit a manipulator, such a master of technique. He adapts with unerring tact his manner to his matter and puts upon us the perfect spell of art. Moreover, even when a reader forces himself to take notice of Poe's artificiality, he may, if he be in the right temper, gain only an added delight, the sort of delight that comes from watching the exquisitely sure play of a painter's firm hand, adapting its action consciously to all the difficulties of its subject. Poe's precocious artistic sophistication is one of his rarest charms for the appreciative amateur. But if a reader be exorbitant and relentless and ask from Poe something more than intellectual resource and technical dexterity, he is pretty sure to be disappointed; Poe has little else to offer him. Doubtless it is Philistinish to ask for this something more; but people have always asked for it in the past, and seem likely to go on asking for it, even despite the fact that Herr Max Nordau has almost succeeded in reducing the request to an absurdity.

CHARLOTTE BRONTË

CHARLOTTE BRONTË was once reproached by the vivacious and ever-confident George Henry Lewes for not more nearly resembling, in her artistic methods, that favourite novelist of the gently cynical and worldly wise, — Jane Austen. Her answering letter, while in tone very prettily submissive, nevertheless justifies vigorously her own methods of writing and her treatment of life. "If I ever *do* write another book," she says, "I think I will have nothing of what you call 'melodrama'; I *think* so, but I am not sure. I *think*, too, I will endeavour to follow the counsel which shines out of Miss Austen's 'mild eyes,' 'to finish more and be more subdued'; but neither am I sure of that. When authors write best, or, at least, when they write most fluently, an influence seems to waken in them, which becomes their master, — which will have its own way, — putting out of view all behests but its own, dictating certain words, and insisting on their being used, whether vehement or measured in their nature; new-moulding characters, giving unthought-of turns to incidents, rejecting carefully elaborated old

K 129

ideas, and suddenly creating and adopting new ones."

These words of Miss Brontë's carry with them a flash from eyes very different in quality from "Miss Austen's mild eyes," and they express more than a passing mood of protest. Charlotte Brontë really believed in her dæmon. She had the faith which so many romantic poets from Blake to Shelley have confessed to, that her words and images were, not cleverly devised, but inevitably suggested. Novelists do not often take themselves so seriously, at least in public, particularly novelists who keep so sanely near the world of fact as Charlotte Brontë keeps. Your Poe and your Hoffmann may professedly dream out and set down their wildly fantastic tales with the same visionary glibness with which Coleridge wrote *Kubla Khan*. But the noteworthy fact is that Charlotte Brontë lays claim to much this same sort of inspiration for her narratives of actual Yorkshire life. Her visions of characters and incidents must have mastered her like veritable hallucinations to lead to such a claim; and this visionary eye of hers may well account, at least in part, for the astonishing vividness of her narratives and for their success in again and again imposing themselves for moments on our faith with a thoroughness that the more sophisticated art of to-day rarely attains. Charlotte Brontë has something of the seer's persuasiveness; she captures our faith at unawares.

In the letter already quoted Charlotte Brontë, while commenting on Jane Austen's work, puts to Lewes a very pertinent question. "Can there be a great artist," she asks, "without poetry?" She herself believed not, and her novels are from first to last faithful illustrations of her creed. It was not for nothing that she lived for so many years a lonely, introspective life between an overcrowded graveyard and the desolate expanses of the Yorkshire moors. The world, as she conceived of it, was not the world of conventional intrigue in drawing-rooms or pump-rooms or gossiping country-side towns; and the news of the world that she sent out through her novels was news that had come to her not by hearsay or tittle-tattle, or authenticated by painstaking watchfulness in the midst of tea-drinkers and scandal-mongers, but news that could bear the comment of the sweep of the moors by day and of the host of stars by night. She was a lyrical poet, and in each of her novels she set herself the task, or rather, her whole energy went into the task, of re-creating the world in such guise that it should have something of the intrinsic beauty of poetry conferred upon it.

Her interpretation of life was, first of all, a woman's interpretation. This is, of course, the conventional thing to say of Charlotte Brontë; but here, as so often, the conventional thing is the true thing, merely in need of a little exposition. Her novels are not feminine readings of life simply in the sense of portraying the passion of love from a woman's point of view. This she does, to be sure, with a power and a beauty that George Eliot, for example, with her impersonal point of view and her withering sense of the rights of intellect, never attains to. But vibrant Jane Eyrism is far from being the sole staple out of which Charlotte Brontë's novels are wrought. Intense sympathy with human love in all its myriad forms, together with an audacious belief in its power to bring happiness, or something better than happiness, *is*, one is tempted to assert, that sole staple. She has an obsession of reckless faith in the worth of love, and from first to last her novels are full of the pathos of craving hearts, and of the worth that life gains when their craving is contented. It is in the tenderness and strength of her loyalty to love in all its guises, and in her delicate perception and brave portrayal of all the fine ministrations of love to life, that the peculiar feminine quality of her novels resides.

For Charlotte Brontë, the struggle for life is the struggle for affection. There is a pathetic uniformity in the development of her stories when one stops to analyze them. In each, some creature striving for happiness is the central controlling character, and the plot of the story is the process by which this needy pensioner of the author is ultimately made heir to unexpected stores of ap-

preciation and sympathy and love. Jane Eyre, at
the opening of her history, is a tragically isolated
little figure, without a sincere friend in the world,
and symbolically busy over a woodcut of the
lonely and frigid arctic regions. At the close,
she has three excellent cousins—the two girls
are as good as sisters; she casually gets, at
the same time with her relatives, a very decent
fortune; and above all, she falls heir to the vast
hoard of passion long secreted in the caverns of
Rochester's heart. Lucy Snowe in *Villette* has much
the same fate; after long months or years of loneliness, she gets back old friends who are thrice as
friendly as before; and the story of *Villette* is
simply the history of Lucy's search for sympathy
and of her acquisition of Monsieur Paul. The
same is true of *Shirley;* the reader's vital interest
in the story depends on his wish to see Caroline
Helstone, Shirley, and Louis Moore duly fitted
out with their fair share of love: Caroline wins
a mother and a lover in a month; and Shirley also,
as the reader doubtless remembers, fares sumptuously at the last. It is droll to note how little
any of Charlotte Brontë's heroines care for literature or art. She herself was apparently hungry
for fame as a writer, but all her heroines are lovers
of life, and of life only; not one of them so much
as coquets with art or literature except as she may
write "exercises" for some favourite master. Very
un-modern are all these young women, and the

young men, too, for that matter, with no subtle dilettante theories, no morbid contempt for life, no erratic veins of enthusiasm or strange kinds of faculty or of genius. They are all simply bent on getting happiness through love of one sort or another.

Dorothea Brooke and her abstract ideal enthusiasm, Charlotte Brontë could not have conceived or created, any more than she could have traced out with relentless sociological and psychological detail the revenge that the "world" took on Dorothea for her fine passion of unconventionality. Not that Charlotte Brontë was less brave in her contempt of cheap worldly standards than George Eliot; but Dorothea's spiritual restlessness and ambition sprang from a complexity of moral and mental life that Charlotte Brontë's culture was too narrow to have suggested to her, and involves a passion for subtler kinds of goodness than Charlotte Brontë's simple, intense nature brought within her ken. Jane Eyre, when waxing discontented with the tameness of her early life at Thornfield Hall, describes her longing to get away in search of "other and more vivid kinds of goodness." *More vivid kinds of goodness* than those that the common run of mortals reach — these Charlotte Brontë ardently believed in and portrayed. Much of the permanent power of her stories comes from the "impetuous honesty" (to quote from Thackeray's characterization of her), and the fiery inten-

sity of imagination with which she puts before
even readers of the present day her sense and
vision of what life may be made to mean for those
who will live sincerely and resolutely. There is
something elemental in her. She gives a new
zest to life like the encounter with a bit of wild
nature, — with a sea-breeze or the tense germinat-
ing silence in the depths of a wood. But she is
elemental at the cost of being primitive, — primitive in her devotion to a few great interests, and in
her lack of refining complexity of thought. Hence
one's sense in reading her that one is moving in a
world remote from the present. Her heroines
indulge in no self-analysis, have no quarrels with
their consciences, no torturing doubts about duty,
no moral or spiritual struggles. They are curiously
definite and resolute little persons, who at every
crisis know in a trice just where duty lies and just
what they want to do. Their minds are clear, their
ideas about what makes life worth while are certain, their wills are intact; their only quarrel is
with circumstance. They have no wish to play
with life imaginatively, no sense of the cost of
committing themselves to a single ideal, no critical
fear of the narrowing effects of action. What
would Charlotte Brontë have made, one wonders,
of Marie Bashkirtzeff ?

Life itself, then, not fancies or speculations about
life, — life of an almost primitive intensity, — is
what Charlotte Brontë's novels still offer to

readers of to-day who may be surfeited with intellectual refinements of thought and feeling. Doubtless there is in her work something of the romantic false preference for savagery and barbarism over civilization, and of the romantic inclination to confuse crudeness with strength. She loathes conventional life and commonplace characters, and her art has to pay the penalty through growing now and then melodramatic and absurd. Her heroes, notably Rochester and Monsieur Paul, cannot always get themselves taken seriously. Their grotesqueness is overaccentuated. They seem to study oddity. They drape themselves in extravagance as in a mantle. But although Miss Brontë's romantic bias — her fondness for the strange — may now and then distort the action and the characters of her stories, she never, unless rarely in her last novel, *Villette*, offends in her own style. She never rants; her taste is sure. Even in describing the most exciting scenes, her style has no strut and no stridency. And so it is easy to forgive the occasional grotesqueness of her incident and to yield to the sincerity of her art. Her romances deal with confessedly exceptional states of passion, — with almost such passions as a lyrical poet might deal with. And the imaginative truth and the beauty of phrase with which she realizes the moods of her heroines — moods which have the beat of the heart behind them, and are not mere fancies of brain-sick dilettantes — give to

many passages in her stories almost the splendour
and power of lyrical poetry.

It used to be said of Dante Gabriel Rossetti that
life was, with him, always at a crisis. Much the
same thing is true of Charlotte Brontë and of her
heroines. Her novels — and this, when one stops
to consider, helps largely to give them their peculiar
tone — are perpetually busy with emotional crises;
they are bent on portraying just the feverish ex-
pectation, the poignant grief, the joy, the glow of
passion, which some special moment or incident
stirs in the heart of the heroine. Very often the
moods that colour her fiction are moods of anxiety,
of breathless waiting, of nervous suspense. Jane
Eyre's moods are continually of this sort. "I
shall be called discontented," she says in one place.
"I could not help it; the restlessness was in my
nature; it agitated me to pain sometimes. Then
my sole relief was to walk along the corridor of the
third story, backward and forward, safe in the
silence and solitude of the spot."

Early and late in *Jane Eyre*, these moments of
eager waiting, sometimes for a definite sorrow or
joy or excitement, sometimes merely with poignant
longing for change, are described fully and vividly.
When Jane, still a wee girl, has to make a start
by coach before break of day for a distant school,
the childish, half-haggard worry of the early morning is not taken for granted, but is put before the
reader with almost oppressive truth. Jane's drive,

many years later, across the country to Thornfield
Hall, and her tremulous sensitiveness meantime to
every new impression, — these also are keenly
realized and faithfully reproduced. Throughout
the story, wherever she is, Jane is continually
aware of the sky-line and half-consciously quarrelling with the horizon. At Thornfield she often
climbed to the leads of the Hall and "looked out
afar over sequestered field and hill, and along dim
sky-line," and "longed for a power of vision which
might overpass that limit." And earlier, at Lo-
wood, she speaks of "the hilly horizon," and adds:
"My eye passed all other objects to rest on those
most remote, the blue peaks; it was those I longed
to surmount."

Lucy Snowe, whose fortunes make up the story
of *Villette*, is not quite so fiery a young parti-
cle as Jane Eyre; but she has almost as many
moods of thrilling restlessness to tell about. Her
nerves vibrate to the "subtle, searching cry of the
wind"; she answers half-superstitiously to all the
skyey influences; she watches with a breathless
exhilaration the Aurora Borealis, — its "quivering
of serried lances," "its swift ascent of messengers
from below the north star." And so throughout
Jane Eyre and *Villette*, — *Shirley*, as will presently
be noted, is somewhat differently conceived, —
moods of acute and febrile intensity are imaginatively put before us. We are kept perpetually
within sound of the heroine's breathing, and are

forced to watch from hour to hour the anguished
or joyful play of her pulse. The moods are not
difficult moods, or subtly reflective moods ; they are
not the ingenious imitations of feelings which the
pseudo-artistic temperament of to-day vamps up to
while away the time and in emulation of the woes
of special souls. They are the veritable joys and
sorrows of eager and keenly sensitive natures that
are bent above all upon living, and that never think
of posing, or of mitigating the severity of life by
artistic watchfulness over their own experiences.
They are primitive, elemental, tyrannical emotions,
and not to be disbelieved.

Another source of the almost lyrical intensity
which runs through Charlotte Brontë's fiction is
her sensitiveness to natural beauty. She had all
a romantic poet's tremulous awareness of the bright
and shadowed world of moor and field and sky.
Her nerves knew nature through and through and
answered to all its changing moods, and rarely do
her stories, even when the scene is laid in a city,
leave long out of notice the coursing of the clouds,
the sound of the winds, the gay or ominous play of
light and shade through the hours of the day, the
look of the moon at night. The creativeness of
her imagination, its searching inclusiveness, are not
to be missed. It is a whole new world she gives us;
she is not content with working out for us the acts or
thoughts or looks of imaginary folk who may move
satisfactorily across any sort of conventional stage.

Her imagination is too elemental for this, too vital, includes too much of the universe within its sensitive grasp. Her people are knit by "organic filaments" to the nature they inhabit, and they can be thoroughly and persuasively realized only as their sensitive union with this nature-world which is their home is continually suggested. With the romantic poet, the individual is far more closely dependent on the vast instinctive world of nature for comfort and help and even for the life of the spirit, than on the conventional world of society, to which his relations seem to such a poet more nearly accidental. In her sympathy with this conception of man as intimately communing with the mysterious life of the physical universe, Charlotte Brontë shows once more her romantic bias.

Accordingly, the pages of her novels are full of delicate transcripts of the changing aspects of night and day, as these aspects record themselves on sensitive temperaments — more particularly on the temperaments of her heroines. *Jane Eyre* is perhaps most richly wrought with these half-lyrical impressions of what the earth and the sky have to say to the initiated. Yet, even through the more objective *Shirley*, Charlotte Brontë's love of nature follows her unmistakably, — the hero, Moore, owing his very name to her passion for the wild Yorkshire downs. In *Villette*, the scene is in Brussels; yet Charlotte Brontë's imagination, even when thus circumscribed, will not wholly

give up the world of nature, and Lucy Snowe finds
in the wind, in the sky, in the moon, companion-
able presences whose varying aspects and utter-
ances symbolize again and again her joys or griefs
or wringing anxieties. "It was a day of winter
east winds," she says in one place, "and I had
now for some time entered into that dreary fellow-
ship with the winds and their changes, so little
known, so incomprehensible, to the healthy. The
north and the east owned a terrific influence, making all pain more poignant, all sorrow sadder. The
south could calm, the west sometimes cheer; unless
indeed, they brought on their wings the burden of
thunder-clouds, under the weight and warmth of
which all energy died." Of the moon as well as
the winds, Lucy is strangely watchful; and often
at some crisis in her externally placid but internally
stormy life she describes its splendour or its sadness. So in Chapter xii: "A moon was in the
sky, not a full moon, but a young crescent. I
saw her through a space in the boughs overhead.
She and the stars, visible beside her, were no
strangers where all else was strange; my child-
hood knew them. I had seen that golden sign
with the dark globe in its curve leaning back
on azure, beside an old thorn at the top of an old
field, in Old England, in long past days, just as
it now leaned back beside a stately spire in this
continental capital." Again: "Leaving the radiant
park and well-lit Haute-Ville . . . I sought the dim

lower quarter. Dim I should not say, for the
beauty of the moonlight — forgotten in the park —
here once more flowed in upon perception. High
she rode, and calm and stainlessly she shone. . . .
The rival lamps were dying; she held her course
like a white fate." Finally, a single passage may
be quoted from *Shirley* because of the way it testi-
fies, through the moon's subjugation of the surly
and stormy temperament of old Yorke, to both
the dramatic and the romantic power of Charlotte
Brontë's imagination. Yorke, the brusque and violent Yorkshire squire, riding in the late evening
over the downs with Moore, the hero, has been
betrayed into talk about a woman he had long ago
loved; suddenly he breaks off. "'The moon is up,'
was his first not quite relevant remark, pointing
with his whip across the moor. 'There she is, ris-
ing into the haze, staring at us in a strange red
glower. She is no more silver than old Helstone's
brow is ivory. What does she mean by leaning her
cheek on Rushedge i' that way, and looking at us
wi' a scowl and a menace?'"

Charlotte Brontë's sensitiveness to the sinister
or seductive beauty of the moon, illustrated by
all these passages, may be taken as typical of
her relation to all nature, and of her use of it
throughout her stories. She has an almost transcendental faith in the meaning of natural sights
and sounds; she reproduces them with a glamour
that only a romantic imagination can catch and

suggest; and the unmistakable sincerity of her moods and the lyrical intensity of her interpretations help to give to her novels a peculiarly vivid beauty that the modern instructed, scientific, and faithless novelist can rarely attain to.

Finally, from the primitiveness, good faith, and concentration on essentials that have been noted as characteristic of Miss Brontë, and from her fiercely insistent dramatic imagination, there results the remarkable power and persuasiveness of the really great scenes of crisis in her stories. Perhaps the greatest of these scenes are those that follow Jane's discovery that Rochester's wife is still alive. The seeming truth of these, their air of being personal experiences poignantly remembered, remains marvellous even for the wariest and most modern of readers. No rightly constituted mind can disbelieve in the details of Jane's flight from Thornfield across the moors, in her solitary night on the heath under "the cloudless night-sky," in her sudden glimpse of "the mighty milky way," and her "nestling to the breast of the hill." The end of the flight may well enough seem ludicrously unreal — Jane's lucky discovery of her cousins in their little cottage set in the measureless waste of the moors; plainly there is some tampering here with the world-order, some bribing of fate. But in spite of this jarring of the antiquated mechanism of the plot, — a disillusioning mischance against which we are never quite safe with Miss Brontë — Jane's feelings and sensations, her agonizing disheartenment, her pathetic clinging to nature for comfort and momentary relief, her poignant passing glimpses of the beauty of flowers and. heath and stars and of the freshness of the morning, her growing weakness and half-delirious wanderings, — all these experiences and moods refuse to be disbelieved, and grasp at the very heart of the reader. A few such passages in *Jane Eyre* have almost the burning colour and the self-sufficing vividness of great romantic poems like the *Ancient Mariner*.

The new world, then, into which Charlotte Brontë's imagination inducts the modern reader and of which she makes him free, is a world where casuistry and philosophy are unknown, where they put no mist of abstractions between the reader and the poignant fact. It is a world where love and hate and the few great primary savage passions, of which recent literary folk of the first order fight so shy, are portrayed vigorously and convincingly. It is a world in which the elements, air and earth and water, flash and blossom and ripple, where the clouds ·and the winds, the sun and the moon, are never quite out of mind, and set the nerves a-tingle and put the imagination in play, even of the folk who are shut indoors.

And yet, though life, as Charlotte Brontë portrays it, is so passionate, and though the world is so primitive and elemental, the life that she puts before us

is *actual* life, not a whimsical or fantastic or falsi-
fying counterfeit of life, and the world in which
her characters live and move and have their being,
is the *actual* world, not a mystical dream-region,
beautifully false in its colours and chiaroscuro
and artificially filled like Hawthorne's world, for
example, with omens and portents and moral symbolism. Her characters, too, are real men and
women, not types, not figures in melodrama, not
creatures of one idea, or one humour, or one passion. Doubtless they are not studied with the
minuteness that modern realists use. Yet they
have complex personalities and lead thoroughly individual lives. And they are flashed on the reader's
retina with a vividness of colour and a dramatic
truthfulness and suggestiveness in act and gesture
that modern scientific novels rarely reach. Herein,
perhaps, lies Charlotte Brontë's unique power, —
in her ability to make her stories seem close to
fact and yet strange and almost mystically imaginative. Her hallucinations are sane, and her victims
of passion keep, after all, within the bounds of
reason.

And indeed this is an aspect of Charlotte
Brontë's genius that has not in general been insisted upon sufficiently— her self-control and her
loyalty to reason, in all that is essential, whether
in art or in morals, a loyalty that is none
the less consistent and controlling because it is
half-grudging. As a result of this loyalty she

L

escapes in her stories much of the extravagance
and absurdity that her sisters were led into. In
some respects, Emily Brontë was a greater artist
than Charlotte; she had an intenseness of vision,
and an occasional beauty of image and phrase,
that Charlotte Brontë never quite reaches. The
vividness of some of her scenes and the acrid
intensity of the counterfeit life in *Wuthering
Heights* are beyond anything in *Jane Eyre* or
Shirley. But the work of Emily Brontë is lacking
in the moral and artistic sanity which is characteristic of Charlotte Brontë. *Wuthering Heights* has
here and there greater lyrical beauty and power
than anything that Charlotte Brontë has written.
But Emily Brontë takes us wholly out of ordinary daylight into a region of nightmare horrors.
Dante Rossetti used to say of *Wuthering Heights*
that its scenes were laid in hell, though oddly
enough the places and the people had English
names. The story, too, is illogical and structure-
less, and hence fails to make a lastingly great
impression; it spends itself in paroxysms and
lacks sustained power and cumulative effect.

Charlotte Brontë, on the other hand, is never
completely the victim of her hallucinations. Contemptuous as she may be of "common sense" in
conventional matters, she is never really false to
reason or careless of its dictates in the regions
either of conduct or of art. When all is said, *Jane
Eyre,* the wildest of her stories, is a shining example

of the infinite importance, both in life and in art, of reason. As a story, it is from beginning to end admirably wrought. It moves forward with an inevitableness, a logic of passion, an undeviating aim, that become more and more impressive, the more familiar one is with the novel, and that mark it as the work of a soundly intellectual artist — of an artist who is instinctively true to the organizing force of reason as well as to the visions of a passionate imagination. In spite of its length and wealth of detail, *Jane Eyre* is an admirably unified work of art. Every moment prepares for, or re-enforces, or heightens by way of subsequent contrast, the effect of the tragic complication in the lives of Rochester and Jane Eyre, — the complication in that passion which seeming for the moment about to bring perfect happiness to the dreary existence of the little green-eyed, desolate waif of a woman, finally overwhelms her and seems to have wrecked her life. The steady march of destiny may be heard if one will listen for it; the fate-*motif* sounds almost as plainly as in *Tristan und Isolde*. To give us now and then this sense that we are watching the working out of fate, is the great triumph of the imaginative artist.

To some, this praise of *Jane Eyre* may sound like droll hyperbole, for there are undoubtedly sadly distracting defects in the story which for certain readers, particularly on a first reading, mar irretrievably its essential greatness. The most important of these have already been noted. "The long arm of coincidence" stretches out absurdly in one or two places, and makes all thought of fate for the moment grotesque. The vices and the ugliness of Rochester are dwelt upon with a fervour that suggests an old maid's belated infatuation for a monstrosity. The sempiternally solemn love-making of Jane and Rochester drones its pitilessly slow length along, with no slightest ironical consciousness or comment on the part of the author. These faults and these lapses of taste are undeniably exasperating, but they grow less prominent as one comes to know the story intimately and to feel its strenuous movement and sincerity; and they finally sink, for any reader who has an instinct for essentials, into their true place, as superficial blemishes on a powerfully original work of art.

Of the existence of these defects in *Jane Eyre*, however, Charlotte Brontë was liberally informed by the critics, and in her later stories she guards against them. Both *Shirley* and *Villette* are freer from absurdities than *Jane Eyre;* neither is quite so frankly devout toward the *outré*, and in both a certain insidious humour is cultivated. *Shirley* is a roundabout tribute to Thackeray. The point of view, the method, the tone, are the result of a hero-worshipping study of the novelist to whom *Jane Eyre* was finally dedicated. The story aims to be more a criticism of life than *Jane Eyre*, and

less a personal confession; the point of view is
that of "the author," and the tone is often whimsical or ironical. From the very first page the
style betokens a changed attitude toward life.
The novel is not to be a semi-lyrical record of
moods of hope and grief and revolt and passion
and joy; it is to portray with a certain delicate
and at times ironical detachment the fortunes of a
small group of characters whom the author lov-
ingly but shrewdly watches. The brisk satire at
the expense of the curates is something that lies
quite out of the scope of *Jane Eyre*. The gain
that *Shirley* shows in conscious breadth of outlook
and in confidence of bearing, — in authority, — is
noteworthy. *Jane Eyre* is the work of an audacious solitary dreamer; *Shirley* is the work of an
author who has "arrived," who has made the
world listen, and who feels sure that she has a
right to speak. The monotonous poignancy of
Jane Eyre gives place in *Shirley* to a wide range
of moods; the story moves forward with a buoyant sense of the charm of life as well as with a
half-indignant sense of its daunting and harrowing
difficulty. The author escapes from the tyranny
of a single, somewhat morbid, though courageous,
temperament, and gives us incidents and characters
with more of the checkered light upon them that
ordinary mortals are from day to day aware of.

Shirley takes in, too, more of the light mis-
cellaneousness of life than *Jane Eyre*, — more

of its variegated surface. *Jane Eyre* concentrates all the interest on the struggle of two hearts with fate; *Shirley*, while loyal to the fortunes of a few principal characters, suggests the whole little world of the country-side, through conflict and coöperation with which these characters gain their strength and quality. At least it tries to suggest this world, — a world of curates, rectors, squires, and even labourers. Tea-drinkings and church festivals and labour riots are conscientiously set forth, and in the midst of their bustle and confusion the wooings of Robert Moore and Louis Moore go on.

Yet one has after all but to think of *Middlemarch* to feel how superficial in Charlotte Brontë's novels is the treatment of sociological detail. In *Shirley* the labourers and their riotous attacks on the mill are plainly enough simply used to heighten the effect of the plot; the rioters come in almost as perfunctorily as the mob in a melodrama, and they pass out of view the moment they have served the purpose of giving the reader an exciting scene in which Moore may act heroically, and over which Shirley and Charlotte may feel intensely. The genius of Charlotte Brontë lay not in the power to realize minutely and thoroughly the dependence of character on social environment, but in her power to portray with lyrical intensity the fates of a few important characters. *Shirley* isolates its characters far less than *Jane*

Eyre, — tries to see them and portray them as
more intimately and complexly acted upon by a
great many forces. It is therefore a wiser, saner,
and more modern book than *Jane Eyre.* But in
proportion it loses in intensity, passionate colour,
and in subduing singleness of aim. The interest is
divided; the dreamlike involvement of the reader
in the mist of a single temperament's fancies and
feelings disappears; the peculiar, half-hypnotizing
effect of Jane Eyre's murmurous, monotonous recital vanishes; and in the place of all this we have
a brilliant, often powerful, and undeniably picturesque and entertaining criticism of various aspects
of Yorkshire life, written somewhat after the
method that George Eliot later used much more
skilfully.

In *Villette* Charlotte Brontë returns to the personal point of view and the more lyrical tone.
Lucy Snowe, who is merely a reincarnation of Jane
Eyre, though somewhat less energetic and less
ugly, puts upon us in this story, as Jane Eyre had
put upon us before, the spell of her dream, and
imposes on us the sad or happy hallucinations that
made up her life. In some respects, *Villette* is the
most of a *tour de force* of Charlotte Brontë's novels.
She takes for heroine a plain, shy, colourless school-
teacher; she puts her in the midst of a girl's
boarding-school, and keeps her there pitilessly
from almost the start to the finish of the story;
she makes use of hardly any exciting incident —

the Spectral Nun is a mere picturesque hoax, though her repeated introduction illustrates the weakness for sensationalism in plots that Charlotte Brontë could never quite rid herself of; there are, however, this time no mad wives, no hollow mysterious laughter, no men or women with suspicious pasts. Yet in spite of the commonplace characters and the seemingly dull situations, the story that results holds the reader's interest firmly with its alternate gayety, pathos, and passion. In places it is as poignant as *Jane Eyre*. After all, we mortals are ridiculously sympathetic creatures; it is the fluttering of the human heart that captures us; and Lucy Snowe's heart finds enough excitement in her Belgian boarding-school to justify a great deal of passionate beating.

Villette suffers, however, from a divided allegiance on the part of the author. Her method in the story is plainly a compromise between the egoistic self-concentration of *Jane Eyre* and the professional detachment of *Shirley*. Lucy Snowe is made more speculative, less acridly self-assertive, than Jane Eyre, to the very end that she may note more of the ordinary happenings of life, and set down a more reflective and inclusive record of what goes on about her than the impassioned Jane would have had patience for. As a consequence, *Villette* gains in range but loses in intensity. The fortunes of the Bassompierres, which, in spite of Lucy's loyalty to the charm of these worthy folk, fail to

perturb the reader very deeply, fill far too much
space. In a letter written about the time of the
publication of the novel, Charlotte Brontë laments
the weakness of the character of Paulina, and the
apparent *non-sequitur* that results in the story from
the early importance of the Bassompierres and of
Dr. John, and from their later obscuration by
Lucy's love for the Professor. This flickering
purpose is perhaps the sign of the difficulty the
author met in trying to be objective. The power
to portray the world with passionate truth as seen
through a woman's temperament, — a narrowly exacting and somewhat morbidly self-centred temperament, — this was the peculiar power of Charlotte
Brontë; and in *Jane Eyre* this power found its
perfect expression. In her other novels, though
she wins a greater range, she sacrifices her peculiar
coign of vantage.

It must, then, be admitted with all frankness
that life is not for most people the sort of thing
that Charlotte Brontë represents. The moods that
fill the pages of *Jane Eyre* are no more the common moods with which the ordinary man or
woman looks at life than are the lyrics of *In
Memoriam* like the daily records of a clubman's
thoughts. For most people, life is not perpetually
at a crisis; nor are they all the time yearning intensely for love and sympathy. Petty personal
rivalries and the pleasure that comes from success
in them, silly little vanities that fancy themselves

flattered, cheap bodily delights, a pleased ironical sense of the absurdities of other people, — these are the satisfactions that for half the world redeem the monotony of existence and make it no hardship to go on living; and these are precisely the phases of life that such novelists as Jane Austen delight to depict. Of all these frivolous feelings Charlotte Brontë's account of life contains scarcely a hint. *Shirley* now and then has glimpses of the absurd trivialities that the cynic likes to find and sneer at. But for the most part Charlotte Brontë is as oblivious as Shelley or Wordsworth of the possible delights of irony. Perhaps it is still an open question whether the ironical or the passionately sincere relation to life is the worthier in morals and in art. The imaginations that can reconcile the two are doubtless the most penetrating and potent. Miss Brontë showed that she could appreciate the ironical manner through her warm admiration of Thackeray, — an admiration, however, be it noted that expressly insists on the "sentiment, which, jealously hidden, but genuine, extracts the venom from that formidable Thackeray, and converts what might be corrosive poison into purifying elixir." As for her own work, however, she was too contemptuous of conventionality in all its forms to be a fit interpreter of the Spirit of Comedy.

Indeed, she now and then herself becomes in her art fair game for the Spirit of Comedy, because of

the dulness of her conventional conscience. She
does not always know when the laugh is bound to
be against her. Her heroes often wax silly or
grotesque. Rochester's smile which "he used but
on rare occasions," his " ebon eyebrows," his " precious grimness," his " bursts of maniacal rage," all
his extravagances of look and demeanour, are insisted upon absurdly. Paul Emmanuel's tricks of
manner, his wilfulness, his self-conceit, his fidgeti-
ness, — these are played upon out of all measure,
and described with a fondness that must now and
then seem ludicrous. And so, too, with the peculiarities of Louis Moore; his sardonic self-satisfaction,
his somewhat pretentious iciness of demeanour, his
satanic pride and so on, are made abundantly grotesque through overemphasis. Melodramatic incident, too, Miss Brontë shows a perilous fondness
for. Not easy is it to take seriously the crazy wife
of Rochester, who goes on all fours in an upper
chamber, and now and then sallies forth to set fire
to something or other. Excesses of this sort both
in characterization and in incident are the penalty
that Miss Brontë has to pay for her contempt for
conventional standards and modes of judgment.

Gradually she doubtless came to recognize the
danger involved in her fondness for the abnormal,
and in her distrust of everyday virtues and modes
of life. In her last novel, *Villette*, she tried to be
fair to conventional types of men and women, and
to portray worldly success sympathetically. In Dr.

John Bretton she aims to draw the character of a
well-bred, good-tempered, prosperous gentleman, —
a man in no disgrace with fortune and men's eyes.
And in Paulina she makes a brave effort to depict
sympathetically a pretty and charming young society girl. Both Bretton and Paulina, however, are
mere copperplate nonentities. Miss Brontë herself
laments in one of her letters her failure with Paulina; and John Graham Bretton, the handsome
young doctor at whom Lucy Snowe confesses she
dare not look for fear of being dazzled for a half-
hour afterward, is also a mere figment. Paul Emmanuel is the real hero of *Villette*, — a hero in his
own way as *outré* as Rochester himself. In *Shirley*,
the insufferable Sympsons — Shirley's buckram
uncle and his faultless daughters — together with
Sir Philip Nunnely, the lily-fingered baronet, who
writes sentimental verses, are the only really conventional folk portrayed. The daughters " knew
by heart a certain young-ladies'-schoolroom code of
laws on language, demeanour, etc. ; themselves
never deviated from its curious little pragmatical
provisions; and they regarded with secret, whispered horror all deviations in others." Mr. Symp-
son's god was " the World," as Shirley tells him in
a virago-like speech toward the close of the story.
All these devotees of " correctness " Miss Brontë
detests; " these things we artists hate," as Blake
said of the *Mechanics' Magazine.* And her hatred
of them gives a kind of dissenting bitterness to

parts of her treatment of life, — a false note of
acerbity like that of the professional heretic. This
is another of the penalties she pays for that fervid
unconventionality which was alike her strength
and her weakness.

In morals, her unconventionality will hardly
seem nowadays very startling, although in her
own day there was much head-wagging among
prim persons, male and female, over the vagaries
and frank passionateness of Jane Eyre. Miss
Brontë never pleaded for a moral revolution. She
had no prophetic glimpses of " the modern woman,"
and she neither preached nor implied a gospel of
woman's rights. She makes brisk war on Mrs.
Grundy and on her notions of womanly propriety,
but beyond this she never ventures. She limits
herself expressly in the preface to the second edition of *Jane Eyre*. " Conventionality is not moral-
ity. Self-righteousness is not religion. To attack
the first is not to assail the last. . . . These things
and deeds are diametrically opposed; they are as
distinct as is vice from virtue. Men too often con-
found them; they should not be confounded; ap-
pearance should not be mistaken for truth." Never
does one of Miss Brontë's heroines actually vio-
late a moral law. Jane Eyre is a signal martyr
to the sacredness of received ideas concerning
marriage and divorce; and Rochester has to pay
dearly for his lax notions about the rights of
crazy wives. His Hall is burned and he just

misses burning with it; he finally gets off with
the loss of an arm and an eye and with several months of parboiled suffering. No; Charlotte
Brontë is a relentless little conservative as regards
all the essentials of the moral code. Her ideal for
woman is the traditional domestic ideal freed from
worldliness and hypocrisy, — the domestic ideal
purged of non-essentials and carried to the nth
degree of potency. All her women are merely
fragments till they meet a man they can adore.

Perhaps, however, Shirley may be brought up
as premonitory of the modern woman. In the
"mutinous" Shirley, "made out of fire and air,"
frank and wilful and just a bit mannish, who
parted her hair over one temple, who was not
afraid of a musket, and who managed her own
estate with a pretty air of self-sufficiency — surely,
in *her*, so one is at first tempted to think, there is
a suggestion of the new woman. Yet, after all, the
suggestion is very slight. Shirley wears her man-
nishness merely as a challenging bit of colour. She
is not intellectual; she has no theories; in her
heart of hearts she longs to be bitted and ruled;
in the core of her nature she is very woman of
very woman, delighting in bravado, in playing at
shrewishness, and then in suddenly obeying orders.
She is merely a modern Rosalind masquerading for
a summer's day in doublet and hose.

It nevertheless remains true that in one sense
Charlotte Brontë prepared the way for the crusade

of the modern woman. Her prodigiously vivid portrayal of the endless possibilities of woman's nature in power and passion and devotion inevitably suggests the rights of women to richer fields for the play of their faculties. "Women are supposed to be very calm generally," Jane Eyre exclaims; "but women feel just as men feel; they need exercise for their faculties and a field for their efforts as much as their brothers do; they suffer from too rigid a restraint, too absolute a stagnation, precisely as men would suffer. . . . It is thoughtless to condemn them, or laugh at them, if they seek to do more or to learn more than custom has pronounced necessary for their sex." This passage in *Jane Eyre* is indeed almost revolutionary. And although it cannot readily be paralleled elsewhere in Miss Brontë's writings, the spirit that pervades it, the indignation of its protest against tyrannical and contemptuous limitations of woman's freedom, doubtless runs through all her novels. In this sense she may truly be described as preparing the way for the saner and more generous conceptions of woman and of her relations to man, that are characteristic of our own day.

What is true of Charlotte Brontë's ideas about women is true of her ethics in general. She has no radically new, no really revolutionary, doctrine. The great good in life — she is never weary of praising it and of illustrating its pricelessness —

is pure human affection. Jane Eyre's cry, in a childish outbreak of feeling, is typical of all Miss Brontë's heroines: "If others don't love me, I would rather die than live." Each of her novels, as has already been noted, reduces in the last analysis to a pathetic quest after affection.

Callousness of heart, lack of "true generous feeling,"—this is for Miss Brontë the one fatal defect of character. Not even unflinching devotion to an abstract moral code or to a systematic round of religious observances can excuse in her eyes rigidity of nature and dearth of genuine human affection. Jane Eyre's cousin Eliza has her time parcelled out into ten minute intervals, which she spends day after day with splendid regularity on the same round of duties; yet she is to Jane Eyre, and to Charlotte Brontë as well, *anathema maranatha*, because she is "heartless." St. John Rivers, with whose fate the very last sentences in *Jane Eyre* concern themselves, is a still more striking case in point. He is consumed with religious zeal; he is absolutely sincere in his devotion to the cause of religion. Yet because he sacrifices love to the successful pursuit of his mission, and because he acts from severely conceived principle instead of from warm human feeling, the fiery little author can hardly keep her hand from angry tremulousness while she portrays him. She loathes him because he forgets "the feelings and claims of little people, in pursuing his own large views." Intense

imaginative sympathy with life in all its forms, —
even with animals and with nature, — this is what
Miss Brontë demands of the characters she will
approve. There must be no cheap sentiment; her
heroes are apt to be stern or even ferocious in
manner; but under a wilful exterior there must
be a glowing spirit of human affection ready to
flash out loyally, though capriciously, whenever
there is real need.

And it is because she believes so unswervingly
in the worth of life as ministered to by love, and
because she sets forth with such manifold truth of
detail and such visionary intensity the realities of
life and love, that her novels, in spite of their obvious defects, keep their power, and are even in
some ways doubly grateful in these latter days of
cynical moralizing. She quickens faith in human
nature and in human destiny. She gives the reader
who will readily lend himself to her spell a new
sense of the heights and depths of passion and of
the unlimited possibilities of life. The finical reader
will find in her much to shock him and bring his
hand to his mouth, and the nicely intellectual
reader will be sure that her *naïveté* is by no means
the finally satisfactory relation to life. The ad-
mirers of George Eliot and of Mrs. Ward will carp
at her ethics or at her lack of them. Doubtless,
her characters love love almost selfishly, and seem
to struggle for it with something of the gambler's
greed. George Eliot's analyses of the dangers of

M

the self-centred and wilful pursuit even of love may lead to a much more scientifically accurate sense of the unimportance of the individual man or woman, and of the absurdity of hoping that the world will order itself to suit the needs of a single heart. George Eliot asserted the rights of the social order; Charlotte Brontë asserted the individual. And for that very reason her novels are tonic in these days when gently cynical resignation has become so largely a fashionable habit of mind in literature and art. George Eliot never tells of love at first hand, and always puts a mist of philosophizing and a blur of moral suasion between her readers and any passionate experience she recites. Charlotte Brontë tells of the joy and the terror and the tragedy of love and life with the intense directness of the lyric poet, and hence even the direst sufferings her characters undergo do not daunt or depress the reader, but rather quicken his sense of kinship with all forms of human experience and his realization of the dignity and scope of man's nature. The human will is never at a disadvantage with Charlotte Brontë. The struggle with circumstance and with fate is bitter, often exhausting; yet there is a curious constitutional buoyant courage in her work that more than counteracts any sympathetic sadness the story may for the moment carry with it.

The same lyrical intensity that has been found in Miss Brontë's modes of conceiving life is charac-

teristic of her style.   It is a powerfully imaginative
and at its best an intensely idiomatic style, and its
beauty of imagery and passionate originality make
possible her peculiar poetic re-creation of life.   Her
style has none of the sharp falsetto note that might
be expected from a woman in a passion; in spite
of her fondness for melodramatic incident, Miss
Brontë bridles her tongue and speaks with a terse-
ness, a precision of phrase, and a reticence that
might well serve as models for such modern
masters of sensational fiction as Mr. Hall Caine.
Charlotte Brontë is in very truth an imaginative
artist in prose.   She is loyal to the traditions of
the best English literature.   She has a delicate
sense of the worth of words and of the possible
beauty of sentences and of the charm of the care-
fully-wrought paragraph.   And this instinct for
style is one more reason — and a prepotent one —
why her novels are not going to be speedily swept
into the dust-bins like the thousand and one novels
of the "lady novelists" of to-day, — improvisers
all, ready and slovenly reporters of personal anec-
dote, "*femmes qui parlent.*"

Charlotte Brontë's style varies sensitively from
novel to novel.   In *Jane Eyre* it is nervous, eager,
staccato, impassioned.   Its tone is curiously personal and intimate.   One of the last chapters
begins — "Reader, I married him."   This half-
appealing, confidential note sounds often through
the story, which may almost be described as a long

series of strangely minute and frank confessions
murmured to the reader in Jane Eyre's own voice,
— in "that peculiar voice of hers," to quote from
Rochester, "so animating and piquant, as well as
soft." In *Shirley* the style is gayer, brisker, less
personal, more professional, more audacious, more
satirical. In *Villette* there is a return toward the
introspective and intensely emotional style of *Jane
Eyre*, but the tone is less vibrant with feeling,
more reflective and observantly amused. And
partly, doubtless, as a result of the author's success
and sense of responsibility, the vice of fine writing
appears in this last of her novels. Repeatedly she
writes *at* her readers, expatiates on art or on other
abstract topics, and in a few instances even in-
dulges in over-rhapsodical passages of sentimental
description. Yet, in spite of these lapses, *Villette*
contains as many memorable phrases and images
as *Jane Eyre* or *Shirley*.

In all her novels alike, her style is exquisitely
specific; it gives us a great deal of the surface of
life — of the aspect both of characters and dramatic
scenes and of nature. Lucy Snowe somewhere
boasts of her liking for "nice details"; she caught
this fancy from her creator. Charlotte Brontë
always has flashingly present in her mind the shapes
and the contours of the world and all the phases of
the dramatic action that she describes. The truth
of her transcripts from nature has already been
illustrated. She is "one of those for whom the

visible world exists." She has seen and loved the
colour-schemes of spring and autumn and winter,
and of morning and evening. "It was a still
night — calm, dewy, cloudless; the gables turned
to the west, reflected the clear amber of the horizon
they faced; the oaks behind were black; the cedar
was blacker; under its dense, raven boughs a
glimpse of the sky opened gravely blue; it was
full of the moon, which looked solemnly and
mildly down on Caroline from beneath that sombre
canopy." . . . "All the hot summer day burned
away like a Yule-log; the crimson of its close
perished; I was left bent among the cool blue
shades, over the pale and ashen gleams of its
night." Nor is she merely finely observant of
the hues and tints that play over the surface
of the great earth-ball and the crystal sphere of
the heavens; she knows the moods which these
colour-chords can send vibrating across sensitive
nerves, and these moods she suggests with great
beauty of phrasing.

Her style is prevailingly an imaginative style;
images continually spring to her lips to express
moods or to suggest the peculiar charm of the
life that she portrays. In *Villette* the heroine
speaks of "the strange necromantic joys of fancy"
that were hers; these necromantic joys Charlotte Brontë herself knew well; they cast flickering lights and shadows across many of her
pages. Yet this hardly suggests, after all, the

fervour and gravity of her most characteristic
imaginative prose. She is not playful; she is not
whimsical; she is strenuous and sombre; or she
is tremulously eager in welcoming and treasuring
in words some serious splendour that nature or
human passion reveals . to her. Passages enough
have already been quoted to illustrate the power
and beauty of her imaginative interpretation of
nature. But one or two more passages may be
adduced to illustrate her treatment of passion, —
the unfaltering and flawless sincerity, and the
sombre intensity of phrase with which she describes it. Take, for example, the paragraphs that
recite Jane Eyre's first moments of suffering when
she finds she must abandon Rochester : —

"One idea only throbbed life-like within me
— a remembrance of God: it begot an unuttered
prayer: these words went wandering up and down
in my rayless mind, as something that should be
whispered; but no energy was found to express
them —

"'Be not far from me, for trouble is near: there
is none to help.'

"It was near: and as I had lifted no petition to
Heaven to avert it, — as I had neither joined my
hands, nor bent my knees, nor moved my lips, — it
came: in full heavy swing the torrent poured over
me. The whole consciousness of my life lorn, my
love lost, my hope quenched, my faith death-struck,
swayed full and mighty above me in one sullen

mass. The bitter hour cannot be described: in truth, 'the waters came into my soul; I sank in deep mire; I felt no standing; I came into deep waters; the floods overflowed me.'" The same sombre splendour that illuminates this long lyrical passage glows out often in a single image. "The human heart can suffer. It can hold more tears than the ocean holds waters. We never know how deep — how wide it is, till misery begins to unbind her clouds, and fill it with rushing blackness." Again and again Charlotte Brontë puts in a single sentence a vivid and beautiful impression of nature with a delicacy of perception and a sureness of phrasing that show how essentially poetic was her genius. "The wind sighed low in the firs: all was moorland loneliness, and midnight hush." Moore "wore a countenance . . . like a still, dark day, equally beamless and breezeless." "He met her with caution, and replied to her in his softest tones, as if there was a kind of gossamer happiness hanging in the air which he feared to disturb by drawing too deep a breath." "The rain is over and gone, and there is a tender shining after it." "That morning I was disposed for silence; the austere beauty of the winter day had on me an awing, hushing influence. That passion of January, so white and so bloodless, was not yet spent; the storm had raved itself hoarse, but seemed no nearer exhaustion." Such sentences as these are charged with beauty, and are almost as full of delight for the lover of style as a lyric poem. The romantic glamour, too, of most of them can hardly be missed.

The peculiar play of Charlotte Brontë's imagination must now be apparent. Romantic she is in the sense that she makes the world over in terms of intense personal emotion. Life as she portrays it is continually stirring with a pathetic unrest; it is wistful, — femininely reaching out after completion. Life is haunted, too; the passing moments are full of presentiments; no single hour is enough to itself; it is nervously aware of change. Her characters are out of the common; their hearts are with them late and soon; the story of their lives is the story of some affection or some passion that succeeds or fails. For the things of the mind her people care only by the way; the same is true, one is tempted to say, of the practical concerns of business, and of the daily routine of conventional human intercourse; these take on meaning and worth only as in retrospect or through anticipation they have some special relation to the drama of feeling which is all the time steadily moving forward. Of this drama, even nature is sensitively aware; the winds have echoes of it, and the moon and the stars are curiously involved in its perturbations. Everywhere the tensely vibrating temperament of the feminine artist constrains us into moods that are by no means those of every day. Of course, there are

tracts in her stories, particularly in *Shirley,* where
the friendly commonplaceness of life is nearer
being recognized, and where the reader comes
closer to watching and listening with the quiet
breathing and the half-amused look of one who
merely observes life's little ironies. But the distinctive tone of Miss Brontë's novels, when one
compares her novels with those of her really great
contemporaries, is of this irresistibly poignant sort.

Yet there is in her stories no faring afar into
the shadowy regions of romance for characters or
background, and no refining away of the substance
of life into fantastic dream-shapes and forms. Her
world has none of the strangeness, the prismatic
variableness, or the mystical dimness and the fugitive magic of Poe's world, and none of the allegorical prescience and duplicity of Hawthorne's
world. She keeps almost as rigorously within the
bounds of the possible as literal-minded novelists
keep; and she is honestly in love with fact, —
with what the wrangle of the creative forces of
nature and society necessitates as opposed to what
the heart delights to dream. Her world is held
together by all the great laws that bind into sane
coherence the physical and the moral world of
sensible folk. And yet her world is an artificially
fashioned world, — a world in which a few interests rule far more persistently and potently than in
the world that most men know; a world in which
the atoms of fact and incident are wrought into

intelligible patterns far more exclusively by the
pulsing energy of human affections than they are
in the prosaic world of ordinary events. Not that
she is a sentimentalist; not that she blinks the
thwarting forces of nature or the cruel tangles in
which human wills involve each other. But she
has magnificent faith in the primal human feelings,
— above all in passion, — and in their power to
justify themselves in the midst of all the dulness, the cruelties, and the tragedies of nature and
society. In terms of this faith and in harmony
with this ideal she creates her mimic worlds. She
is essentially loyal to fact; and yet she finds in
fact, even in cruel and tragic fact, subtle ministrations to the needs of the human heart. And
because she is able to convey to her readers her
peculiar appreciation of the power and the beauty
of life, with the consummate skill of the artist,
she belongs with Mrs. Browning among those who
domicile Romance in the midst of the dull facts
of daily life.

THREE LYRICAL MODES

I

THE last eighteen months in England have given a worthy account of themselves in the matter of verse. Within this period two poets of distinction have made themselves for the first time really known; and another poet, who had for an unhappy interval been silent, has returned to the public with a volume of verse of undeniable quality. The new-comers are, of course, Mr. Francis Thompson and Mr. John Davidson; and the poet who returns to find his welcome more assured than ever, is, equally of course, Mr. William Watson.

Of the younger generation of verse-writers in England, Mr. Watson has, for obvious reasons, won the most favour. He has been longest before the public, has accustomed the English retina to his image, and has lost something of that strangeness of aspect which in England so provokes distrust. Then he has been able to call Mr. Richard Holt Hutton of the *Spectator* "his friend," and has fared sumptuously in that journal after

1 Written in June, 1895.

each of his appearances in print.   Of a recent poem
of Mr. Watson's in the *Yellow Book*, Mr. Hutton
has asserted that it contains a symbol that Milton
never surpassed; and persistently during the last
year the *Spectator* has claimed for Mr. Watson the
right to rank with the greatest English poets.
Indeed, English critical journals in general have
received Mr. Watson's work with a favour that
begets distrust.   And yet it must be admitted that
his popularity has never been of quite that com-
promising sort that, for example, has welcomed Mr.
Lewis Morris, — the God-gifted hand-organ voice of
England. The eulogists of Mr. Watson have been
"people of importance"; people perhaps rather
official and Academic, not to say priggish, but certainly people from whom one differs at one's peril.

Mr. Watson is a loyal Wordsworthian, as was
Matthew Arnold before him, and this fact alone
is enough to have ensured his acceptance with a
wide circle of orthodox English readers of poetry.
Not only are many single poems of Mr. Watson's
plainly reminiscences of Wordsworth, — as, for example, the poem describing the swans that float into
view in visionary fashion down the Thames, trailing
clouds of glory from some unknown, half-mystical
region, — but Mr. Watson's entire spirit, when he is
at his best, is undeniably Wordsworthian.   In his
most characteristic moments, his poetry is an aspiration toward that mood of passionate calm, of
perfectly controlled ardour, which Wordsworth of

all romantic poets most adequately realized and
expressed.

> " 'Tis from those moods in which life stands
> With feet earth-planted, yet with hands
> Stretched toward visionary lands,
>   Where vapours lift
> A moment, and aërial strands
>   Gleam through the rift,

> " The poet wins, in hours benign,
> At older than the Delphic shrine,
> Those intimations faint and fine,
>   To which belongs
> Whatever character divine
>   Invests his songs.

> " And could we live more near allied
> To cloud and mountain, wind and tide,
> Cast this unmeaning coil aside,
>   And go forth free,
> The World our goal, Desire our guide, —
>   We then might see

> " Those master moments grow less rare,
> And oftener feel the nameless air
> Come rumouring from we know not where."

The mood pervading these lines is distinctly Wordsworthian, and it is the mood most frequently found
in Mr. Watson. Like Wordsworth, he is always
hearkening for the "intimations" of man's more
than earthly destiny, but the "intimations" in
these later days have become sadly attenuated,
"fainter and finer" than of old; and Mr. Watson's
account of them lacks the "sober certainty" as well

as the spiritual exaltation of Wordsworth's recital, despite his loyalty to the Wordsworthian point of view.

But Wordsworth is by no means the only poet whose influence is traceable in Mr. Watson's work; echoes of Matthew Arnold may be heard again and again. And when one bears these resemblances in mind, and remembers also that Mr. Watson has given an entire poem to the exceptionally delicate and sure appreciation of the best English poets in their long succession, one is forced to admit that whatever else Mr. Watson may or may not be, he is certainly traditional; he has trained himself in the school of the muses; he has formed himself patiently on the best models; he is a loyal cherisher of precedent and good example. And one is furthermore tempted on to the conclusion that in this loyalty to tradition and to precedent is to be found the explanation not only of Mr. Watson's popularity and of the undeniable beauty of much of his verse, but also of what, in the last analysis, proves to be the disappointing quality of his work as a poet, when judged by exacting standards. He has subjected a by no means powerful genius to a training and discipline that have brought him exquisite sureness of taste and deftness of technique, but have failed to develop real richness of nature or any novel or distinctive envisagement of life. He is too much of a poetic sacerdotalist; his authenticity has been his ruin.

Mr. Watson is vaingloriously traditional; he has
the ideal temper for a laureate; he prides himself
openly on being heir to a manner and a "mystery."
His art is intensely sophisticated and almost always
self-conscious. He even boasts in good, set terms
that he is a divinely dowered poet. It seems
strange to find an artist of his unquestionably
fine taste including in his last volume verses as
youthfully self-conscious and arrogant as those on
The Sovereign Poet: —

> " He sits above the clang and dust of Time,
>   With the world's secret trembling on his lip,
>   He asks not converse or companionship
>   In the cold starlight where thou canst not climb."

Of course, Mr. Watson's pose is not often so relentless as this, and yet rarely, indeed, is he quite
unconscious of his mission; he nearly always wears
his rue with a difference.

Traditional, too, are Mr. Watson's *motifs;* and
this is something that can less readily be pardoned
than his traditional manner. In his last volume
there are few important poems in going over which
the reader does not feel that he is on familiar
ground, — ground hallowed by its associations with
many earlier bards. Not that Mr. Watson does not
often give us glimpses of beauty for which we have
to thank primarily his quick poetic eyes; but the
regions themselves through which he takes us have
been for generations sacred to the muses. One of

his favourite contrasts is that between the scope
of human desire and the narrow limits imposed
upon human destiny. This is the old antinomy
which has been poetically expounded in countless
fashions since Byron's day and long before: —

> "But I am fettered to the sod,
>   And but forget my bonds an hour;
>   In amplitude of dreams a god,
>   A slave in dearth of power."

Does not this lament, which the Romanticists and
the post-Romanticists have for so many years versi-
fied for us with so many beautiful modulations,
come to us to-day somewhat belated? So again,
with the poet's beautifully phrased regret as he
watches the flight of a lark.

> "Two worlds hast thou to dwell in, Sweet, —
>   The virginal untroubled sky,
>   And this vext region at my feet. —
>   Alas, but one have I ! "

Here, too, the *motif*, undeniably beautiful as is
its expression, is likely to seem a mere reminiscence. Not that the skylark is itself tabooed; but
the special symbolism the poet finds in its song
is perilously near triteness. In recent years, Mr.
Meredith has heard in the lark's song a more
modern suggestion. Other *motifs* which Mr. Watson elaborates are the sacredness of the poet's
mission, the tragic solemnity of life, the pathos of
the waning belief in immortality, the difficulty of

escaping from old religious formulas, and regret for "the frost-bound, fire-girt scenes of long ago." All these themes are eminently proper, but perhaps not altogether new.

Finally, Mr. Watson is inclined to be morbidly correct in all his doings and sayings, — in his manner as well as in his moods. Passionate calm is the ideal of the true Wordsworthian; aspiration intense in its visionary grasp of the ideal, but nobly restrained in its allegiance to the actual. Unfortunately, with all Wordsworth's disciples the calm and the loyalty to fact have been much easier of emulation than the transcendental fervour that with Wordsworth redeemed and transformed them. In Matthew Arnold the loss of fervour was noticeable enough, and produced that wanness and anæmic pallor that disfigures much of his poetry. In Mr. Watson the poet's self-control has become almost offensively complete; his face never glows or darkens or quivers under the play of passion; often he gives the impression of speaking through a mask.

II

Quite otherwise is it with the work of Mr. John Davidson. To quote from one of his own poems, "old and new" are ever "weltering upon the border of" his "world." He is above all else modern and individual, and the prevailing note of his art is restless sincerity. He is the partially articulate

N

bard of a new world in the process of making.
Doubtless these merits carry with them certain
countervailing defects. His passion is often turbid
and uncontrolled, and considering his age — Mr.
Davidson must now be thirty-five — he still finds
certain of the commonplace evil tricks of life
strangely novel and exasperating; one would think
that the poet would have sooner grown used to the
laws of the game. But at any rate he is intensely
alive; he is "part of all that he has seen" and
experienced in this age of contending ideals, of
perishing creeds, and slowly evolving systems.
Everywhere he grasps uncompromisingly the rudest
facts of modern civilization, — facts material, industrial, social, and religious, — and his imagination is, at its best, compelling enough and his power
of enjoyment, rich enough to enable him to find
in these forbidding externalities an essential spirit
of beauty, which he knows words to evoke. The
stacks of a factory town that "lacquer the sooty
sky," the shrieks of steam whistles "that pipe the
morning up before the lark," the telegraph wire
"taut and lithe, within the wind a core of sound,"
the train, a "monster taught to come to hand
amain," — these and similar modern corruptions
because of which Mr. Ruskin refuses to be com-
forted, simply challenge Mr. Davidson's virile imagination and put it into fierce play in the service of
a brave love of life. Humanity in all its forms,
forbidding as well as alluring, sends currents of

sympathy through his veins, and sets him to a swift fashioning of dramatic scenes and a loving portrayal of motive and mood. He has felt the tragic fate of the wretchedest of respectabilities, the clerk "at thirty bob a week," and has celebrated the courage with which this starving victim of the English social system suffers stanchly till he falls in his place; it is British pluck in its protoplasmic form of which he here sings the praise and illustrates the indomitableness. Nothing modern is foreign to Mr. Davidson, and some of his best effects are secured from the most sordid material.

In his relation to religion, Mr. Davidson is also "modern"; but here the peculiar form of his modernity is hardly so attractive. Some one has dubbed him, because of his treatment of religious themes, "the man who dares." But his daring seems to many to be rather uninstructed and flaunting. In his *Exodus from Houndsditch*, for example, he describes a wild phantasmagoria of woe, — "women on fire! and tortured girls and boys!" — and attributes all the suffering, with no hint of compensating good, to the Christian religion. This utterly unhistorical conception is the favourite one with those who have been used to look up to the late Mr. Bradlaugh and Mr. Ingersoll as men of light and leading, but seems a bit surprising in a man of Mr. Davidson's literary attainments. In *The Ballad in Blank Verse of the Making of a Poet*, religion is assailed with the

same virulence; the severities and strenuous spirituality of Christianity are contrasted in true Swin-
burnian fashion with the luxuriant beauty and
frank, sensuous splendour of Hellenism: ultimately,
however, the poet turns from both Christianity and
modern Paganism to what seems to him a still more
modern mood, in which he gives over the attempt
to formulate truth, whether religious or moral, and
accepts all life indifferently as worthy of passionate
sympathy and imaginative expression.

> " No creed for me ! I am a man apart:
> A mouthpiece for the creeds of all the world ;
> A soulless life that angels may possess
> Or demons haunt, wherein the foulest things
> May loll at ease beside the loveliest ;
> A martyr for all mundane moods to tear."

Surely, this is a shallow and ranting account of
the irresponsibility of the artist; it is dilettantism "without the manner's charm," — dilettantism
grown violent and raucous. Not in these poems,
nor indeed in any of his poems, does Mr. Davidson
show that he has done much thinking or got at
what life means except as far as his senses or his
feelings can tell him.

In still another way religion enters often into Mr.
Davidson's poetry. He is fond of using the symbols, the names, the terms of Christianity for purely
decorative effect. In his *Ballad of Heaven* and
his *Ballad of Hell* and *Ballad of a Nun* Satan,
the Virgin Mary, and even God the Father appear

as actors. Yet the action is always palpably make-believe; the stories exist solely as stories, and have at the utmost merely an allegorical value. The strange point is to find this tendency to treat Christianity as a beautiful myth existing side by side with such intense hatred of the system as Mr. Davidson elsewhere expresses, and also side by side with such ethical sincerity as he shows in much of his writing. In Dante Gabriel Rossetti's poetry, also, Christianity fades into a series of beautiful myths; but it suffers this transformation, only with everything else that enters the "dreamland vaporous and unaccountable" of Rossetti's mind. Rossetti never cares for anything outside his dream. Mr. Davidson sympathizes intensely with the feelings of all those whose world he shares; hence the strangeness of finding so vital a system as Christianity, becoming to him merely a means of fitting himself out with the paraphernalia of art.

And yet, after all, coherence is not specially the habit of Mr. Davidson's mind. In his narrative poems he carries to its extreme the balladist's right to move by leaps and bounds. In the *Ballad of a Nun* the action is only sublimated hysteria, and the actors, Virgin Mary and all, are merely irresponsible degenerates. Doubtless the moral of this Ballad and of the Ballads of Heaven and of Hell, is Love Triumphant. But to the prosaic mind Love as hymned by this very modern poet of the

London streets seems rather a destroyer than a
saviour or regenerator.   Love helps Mr. Davidson's heroes and heroines to go through some very
picturesque paroxysms, and there the matter ends.

When all is said, however, Mr. Davidson's work
has an intense vitality that justifies it in spite of
minor faults.   Such a poem as the *Ballad in Blank
Verse* pulses with the poet's blood from the first
line to the last.   Mr. Davidson lives in his poetry
from moment to moment with a passion and a
fierceness of conception and an intimacy of relation
to the facts of the time that can hardly be matched
in any of the younger poets.

III.

To Mr. Francis Thompson we certainly must not
look for any similar valorous attempt to bring all
life within our scope and to find everywhere aspects
of beauty.   Not that he does not offer us beauty
abundantly and unstintedly.   Whatever is within
the range of his sympathy, whatever kindles his
imagination, forthwith becomes in his verse mystically beautiful beyond anything that Mr. Watson
or Mr. Davidson has power to produce.   But his
spirit lives within a magic crystal sphere, which
gives entrance to but few of the commonplace
objects of modern life and holds afar, dimly in-
effectual, its crass immediacy and bewildering
insistence of appeal, and its coarse and glaring

disorder. It is as the poet of an inviolate region of intense personal emotion that Mr. Thompson is specially distinguished.

Mr. Thompson's rhythms are much subtler and more varied and vital than those of our other two poets and mark him at once as preëminently a singer. Mr. Davidson in *Ballads and Songs* never escapes from iambics, and Mr. Watson in his last volume exchanges them only once for measures of another kind. Mr. Thompson's poetry is not simply rich in trochaic and anapæstic and dactylic measures, but is full of the most delicate metrical *nuances*, where from phrase to phrase, and verse to verse, the rhythm vibrates more slowly or swiftly in intimate response to the play of feeling and imagination.

Mr. Watson's verse is "frozen music"; Mr. Thompson's, the exquisitely modulated utterance of a flexible, vibrant voice. In his poetry, words lose their hard, individual outlines; speech is no longer merely a series of conventional signs which are put together mechanically in accordance with recognized laws; sound becomes a new art medium, created from moment to moment, continuous in its subtle effects of contrast and correspondence, end-lessly suggestive in its changing tone-colours and emotional perturbations, magical and inexplicable in its power to transfer a new mood from the heart of the poet, the master of moods, to the heart of the reader. This is, of course, what language be-

comes in the poetry of every great artist; but in
the poetry of Mr. Thompson, far more impressively
than in that of most modern versifiers, language
undergoes this imaginative regeneration or re-
creation, and becomes vitally suggestive in numberless novel ways. He is less at the mercy of individual words than either Mr. Davidson or Mr.
Watson; he works in larger sound-masses, and
confers upon sound a subtler and more penetrating symbolic suggestiveness. These phases of his
genius can hardly be illustrated by means of extracts; yet some glimpses of the music and beauty
of his verse may be caught from a stanza or two of
The Making of Viola.

I.

The Father of Heaven.

" Spin, daughter Mary, spin,
   Twirl your wheel with silver din ;
   Spin, daughter Mary, spin,
   Spin a tress for Viola.''

Angels.

" Spin, Queen Mary, a
   Brown tress for Viola.''

II.

The Father of Heaven.

" Weave, hands angelical,
   Weave a woof of flesh to pall —
   Weave, hands angelical —
   Flesh to pall our Viola.''

Angels.

" Weave, singing brothers, a
   Velvet flesh for Viola.''

And so the verses go on, tremulously tender in
their modulations and evanescent in their shifting
tone-colours, through their archaic progressions of
harmony. Much simpler, but in its own way
equally suggestive, is the music of the first of
the *Poems on Children:* —

> " Her beauty smoothed earth's furrowed face !
>   She gave me tokens three :
> A look, a word of her winsome mouth,
>   And a wild raspberry.

> " A berry red, a guileless look,
>   A still word, — strings of sand !
> And yet they made my wild, wild heart
>   Fly down to her little hand.

> " For standing artless as the air,
>   And candid as the skies,
> She took the berries with her hand,
>   And the love with her sweet eyes.

> *   *   *   *   *

> " She looked a little wistfully,
>   Then went her sunshine way :
> The sea's eye had a mist on it,
>   And the leaves fell from the day."

Such delicate and airily drifting effects, however,
are only a small part of those that Mr. Thompson
is master of. His richer and more intricate harmonies are to be found in *A Judgment in Heaven*,
To Monica Thought Dying, and *The Hound of
Heaven*. For breadth and splendour of metrical

effect, varied with delicate interludes of quieter beauty, *The Hound of Heaven* is not to be matched in recent years, except in the volumes of Mr. Swinburne; and it has a sincerity and undecorative truth of tone, that Mr. Swinburne's verse is apt to lack. *A Judgment in Heaven* also is remarkable for its metrical audacity; in elaborateness of rhythm and gorgeousness of tonal effects it suggests the methods and colour-schemes of the most picturesque modern orchestral pieces.

A Judgment in Heaven calls up at once the charge so often urged against Mr. Thompson, that he is affected and artificial. Without doubt, certain of his poems are curiously reminiscent of the Metaphysical Poets, — of Donne and of Cowley. In *Her Portrait*, for example, mediæval essences and abstractions, of the kind that abound in the works of poets for whom scholastic theology was more than a name, are oddly in evidence, and we hear a great deal of such entities as "encumbering virility," "loveliness corporeal," "prison of femineity," and so on. The mythology, too, and the decorative allusions in such poems are continually Biblical and add to the mediæval effect; the ingenuity of the play with imagery is often of Cowleian quaintness or has the wayward splendour and subtle suggestiveness of Donne.

> " God laid his fingers on the ivories
> Of her pure members as on smoothèd keys,
> And there out-breathed her spirit's harmonies."

The delight in conceits and in a strange, tricksy manipulation of words recalls the manner of the seventeenth century poets: —

> " Herself must with herself be sole compeer,
> Unless the people of her distant sphere
> Some gold migration send to melodise the year.
> But first our hearts must burn in larger guise,
> To reformate the uncharitable skies,
> And so the deathless plumage to acclimatise."

For a few readers even the super-subtlety and the wilful over-refinement of such passages will have an archaic charm; but it should be noted that this mannerism almost disappears in the later poems of the volume.

On the other hand, ornateness of phrasing, a certain ventriloquence of style, an attempt to gain impressiveness for the voice by making it reverberate through high-sounding words from an undetermined distance, — this remains characteristic of Mr. Thompson even in some of his very latest poems. In *A Judgment in Heaven*, for example, he describes " a grisly jaw " of clouds " whose verges supportlessly congest with fire, and suddenly spit forth the moon." We feel like exclaiming with Maria in *Twelfth Night*, — " Lo, how hollow the fiend speaks within him." Yet even in such passages there is something more than grandiloquent diction; there is always rich imagery, faithfully conceived, though perhaps needlessly elaborated and over-ornamental. Moreover, the imagery is vital

and novel, and not of a conventional pattern like
that into which another great master of language,
Mr. Swinburne, is sometimes betrayed. Although
Mr. Thompson is doubtless a virtuoso of the dic-
tionary, and at times seems simply exhibiting his
technical command of its pages, yet in fact his
imagination in nearly every case keeps pace with
his phrasing, and his radical fault in showy passages is, perhaps, after all not so much luxuriance
of language as extravagance of imagery.

As a seer of visions Mr. Thompson is by all odds
the greatest of the younger poets. His imagination
is far-ranging in its scope, intensely brilliant in its
colouring, and penetrative and renovating in its
interpretations. Interstellar distances and celestial
magnitudes do not daunt him more than they
daunted Shelley; "the blue regions of the air" and
the "planetary wheelings" of the heavens are
known to him in all their vicissitudes, and haunt
his imagination with their symbolic suggestions.
He has himself rather daringly described with a
phrase and an image the flashing scope of his vision
and the range and strength of his imagination,
where in *The Hound of Heaven* he speaks of

"The linked fantasies in whose blossomy twist
   I swung the earth a trinket at my wrist."

The hyperbole, audacious as it is, does not seem
beyond bounds as one reads Mr. Thompson's most
characteristic poems and follows the rapid and sure

questing of his imagination. Not since Shelley has
imagery had a finer cosmic scope and magnificence
of colour than in the following passages: —

"I dimly guess what time in mists confounds;
Yet ever and anon a trumpet sounds
From the hid battlements of Eternity,
Those shaken mists a space unsettle, then
Round the half-glimpsed turrets slowly wash again."

*   *   *   *   *   *

"The calm hour strikes on yon golden gong,
    In tones of floating and mellow light
A spreading summons to even-song:
        See how there
        The cowlèd night
Kneels on the Eastern sanctuary stair.
What is this feel of incense everywhere?
Clings it round folds of the blanch-amiced clouds,
    Upwafted by the solemn thurifer,
The mighty spirit unknown,
That swingeth earth before the embannered Throne?"

*   *   *   *   *   *

"This labouring, vast, Tellurian galleon,
Riding at anchor off the orient sun,
Had broken its cable, and stood out to space
Down some frore Arctic of the aërial ways:
And now, back warping from the inclement main,
Its vaporous shroudage drenched with icy rain,
It swung into its azure roads again;
When, floated on the prosperous sun-gale, you
Lit, a white halcyon auspice, 'mid our frozen crew."

The unconscious courage of such passages as these,
their successful audacity, their adequacy of vision,
imaginative integrity, and largeness of utterance,

above all the unhalting and inborn ease of manner with which great things are wrought before our eyes, compel recognition of Mr. Thompson's originality and power as a creative artist.

In the intensity and the quality of his passion, as well as in the scope and vividness of his imagination, Mr. Thompson is, among the younger poets of to-day, preëminent. Mr. Watson, when compared with him, is wan and conventional, and Mr. Davidson turbulent and murky. The magnifying and transforming power of passion, its way of exalting or intensifying trifles till they overshadow the soul intolerably or pierce it irreparably, has rarely been better portrayed than in the poem *To Monica Thought Dying*. The quaint words that the child had last used in whimsical comradeship with her older friend, become in the poet's mind a haunting refrain, tragic because of its incommensurability with the passion of grief that he now tries to express. One would almost have to go to *King Lear* for a like terrible transformation of "childish babble" and a like overwhelming contrast between the trivial and the tragic. Yet the tone is throughout restrained, despite the passion and the strenuous sweep of the verse. There is no turbulence, no confusion of tongues, no blurring of outlines or shattering of imagery. The world is the world of plastic imagination, where even the most forbidding shapes and awful presences of life grow "beautiful through love."

Beauty, indeed, is the one word with which to greet and to take leave of Mr. Thompson's poetry. Not that he belongs among those who divorce art from life, and seek beauty in disregard of all else. Neither in mood nor in treatment is he to be classed with the devotees of art for art's sake.   His poetry emancipates and strengthens, whereas theirs unnerves, and is evermore "wreathing a flowery band to bind us to the earth."   He gives us the piercing bitter-sweet of myrrh, "like a sorrow having wings," in place of the languorous perfumes of nard of which their verses are redolent.   Beauty there everywhere is in his poetry: but it is beauty spiritual as well as sensuous; beauty quintessential, primordial, regenerative; beauty that stings the spirit into keener activity and more passionate aspiration.

TAINE'S INFLUENCE AS A CRITIC[1]

In March, 1857, Sainte-Beuve devoted two of his *Causeries du Lundi* to the discussion of *Divers écrits de M. H. Taine.* He chose for special analysis Taine's *Essai sur Tite-Live,* his Doctor's thesis on La Fontaine, which was later enlarged and republished, and his *Philosophes classiques du XIXᵉ siècle.* Taine had taken his Doctor's degree only four years before, but he had marked each succeeding year with a work of first-rate importance; he had also published from time to time noteworthy essays on such widely different subjects as Xenophon, Saint-Simon, Guizot, and Mme. de la Fayette. In all these treatises and essays the comparatively unknown author had pleaded for and illustrated new methods and new aims in literary criticism, and despite his youth and inexperience and venturesomeness, his work had shown none of the tentativeness or the weakness of first experiments. It became plainer with each publication that the new critic was a man of genuine power and originality; and Sainte-Beuve, with characteristic grace and generosity, made haste to welcome him.

[1] Published in the *Nation,* on Taine's death, in 1893.

There is something almost dramatic in this first encounter between the two critics.   Sainte-Beuve was the representative of the old tradition in criticism, while Taine was confessedly an innovator. The idealists and the Romanticists who fared so ill at the hands of Taine, had many of them been personal friends of Sainte-Beuve.   The idealistic tradition in literature with which Sainte-Beuve certainly sympathized, however completely he had rid himself of early romantic illusions, was the special object of Taine's contempt and ridicule.   Again, Sainte-Beuve was the literary critic pure and simple; he had coquetted, it is true, with science, but he had never let his coquetries pass beyond the bounds of decorum or affect his professional work. Now it was on science that Taine's whole method was founded; his terminology was drawn from science, and it was in the name of science that he came forward to reform literary criticism.   Therefore, if Sainte-Beuve had in his favour the prestige of a great tradition, Taine on his side had the prestige of a popular catchword, for just at this time science was the cry of the hour, and realism was revenging itself for the romantic excesses of 1830.

Of the tact and skill with which, under these rather exacting conditions, Saint-Beuve acquits himself, there can be but one opinion: they are worthy of the great apostle of good taste.   He recognizes at once Taine's scholarship, his curious maturity, his sureness of touch, his certainty of aim

o

and of method. He speaks pleasantly of the duty
that older men owe to such juniors as really
"count" — that of scanning them well and coming
to know them thoroughly. Moreover, to have to
do with these newest arrivals tends to make you
young again, even though the new-comers show
their youth only by their vigour, and present themselves before you full-grown and full-armed. But
it behoves you to be on your guard and to tighten
your belt as you approach them.

After this gracious and generous greeting, Sainte-
Beuve goes on to make some very searching strictures on Taine's ideas and methods. Under guise
of a tribute to Taine's thoroughness and scholarship, he at once suggests the points in which, he
thinks, Taine most offends against the spirit and
the ideals of good criticism. Taine is too desper-
ately serious : he has the set look and the business-
like bearing of a man in a laboratory, who handles
hot crucibles and deals with dangerous compounds.
And again, he is too disputatious : he is always
bent on proving a thesis; the air of the Sorbonne
lecture-rooms clings about his volumes. These
faults of bearing are for Sainte-Beuve significant of
radical defects of temperament and of method.
Taine does not put himself in touch with his
author; he does not enter sympathetically into the
spirit of the work he criticises; he uses his author
for his own special purposes; he wrests his author's
ideas into illustrations of his own pet theories; or,

as Sainte-Beuve elsewhere puts it, the critic pulls
the blankets all to his side of the bed.

These charges — though charges is too harsh and
criminating a word for the suave insinuations of
Sainte-Beuve — take up a large part of the first
essay.   But here and there in the first essay, and
at still greater length in the second essay, Sainte-
Beuve adopts a different point of view, and with
admirable ingenuity turns Taine's own principles
against Taine himself.   The sum and substance of
the earlier criticisms was that Taine was not an
"appreciator," but a scientific student of literary
forms and an historian of ideas ; Sainte-Beuve's
quarrel was with Taine's whole ideal.   The later
criticisms suggest that Taine is false to his own
ideal; that while he is professing to reform literary criticism in the name of science and to put it
on a scientific basis, he is continually violating the
laws of science and departing from the methods of
scientific investigation.   He is too much of a sys-
tematizer and too ambitious in his ideal construc-
tions ; he is impatient of doubt or uncertainty, and
forges links out of nothing wherever there are
breaks in the chain of his evidence.   In attempting
to sum up an individual under a formula, he sins
against science, by disregarding the infinite complexity of the problem and by using rough-and-
ready methods for solving it.   Before "talents" or
characters can be classed or grouped under formulas, an almost endless series of observations must

be made on all kinds of men and under a vast variety of conditions; to attempt to frame out of hand a few cheap formulas for typical characters is a radically unscientific mode of procedure.

By some of Sainte-Beuve's suggestions Taine undoubtedly profited; in his subsequent work, he insists less dogmatically on the significance of "*la faculté maîtresse*" and on the possibility of finding a single phrase by which to sum up an individual in a formula.   The parable of Adam naming the beasts of the field at the behest of the Lord had had its effect.   Taine's love of system, however, and his general methods of work remained unchanged.   He was still invariably bent on proving a thesis, and he was as far as ever from being satisfied, after the manner of impressionistic critics, with merely dabbling in the standing pool of his feelings.   Of the importance of method in the study of literature and of the value of his own method in its main features, he was as firmly convinced as ever; and his next great work, his *Histoire de la littérature anglaise*, published in 1864, was constructed from first to last in illustration of his method and in obedience to his principles.   In fact, the possibility of a scientific explanation of literature was the specific thesis which in this case Taine nailed up to be proved, and his *History of English Literature* was merely the four volume demonstration of a thirty-page theorem.

Certainly this work of Taine's must always

stand as a superb *tour de force*. It is easy enough to carp at it; to disagree with this or that estimate; to blame the critic for overrating Byron and for doing scant justice to Shelley; to exclaim at the yeoman's service exacted from a few such terms as Berserker rage, Puritan cant, English stolidity; to mock at French prejudice, and to accuse the critic of being mechanical and hard and unsympathetic, of turning everything into demonstration, and of being hypnotized by a theory. But, after the bitterest possible things have been said, it still remains true that the *History* is a magnificent achievement and a work of the greatest possible significance. Merely as a piece of literary engineering, it is a marvel of skill: its books, its chapters, and its sections are massed with a sure eye both for literary effect and for sequences of thought; and the table of contents alone is more stimulating reading than the texts of most histories of English literature. But, of course, what makes the book unique is its thoroughgoing attempt to explain a whole literature in terms of national character, inherited culture, and environment.

Not that the underlying principle on which Taine's method depends had not been enunciated long before. That principle is, of course, the historic continuity and the organic unity of national life; and for the earliest suggestion of that principle and the earliest development of a method

somewhat in harmony with it, we should have to
go back at least to Taine's great countryman, Mon-
tesquieu, whose *Esprit des Lois* was a more or
less conscious attempt to find in all a nation's institutions and activities the expression of one mould-
ing and guiding spirit.   Later on, in the eighteenth
century, the principle was grasped at least partially
by Winckelmann, whose *Geschichte der Kunst des
Alterthums* (1764) recognized the relativity of the
arts, and the essential and necessary connection
between the life of a people and its art-expression.
It was Herder, however, who first realized all that
the principle involved, and undertook to apply it
systematically and in detail to the study of literature.   Literary criticism, in passing into his hands
from those of Lessing, was totally changed in
scope, methods, and aims; it no longer sought to
appraise the æsthetic value of pieces of literature
according as they met or fell short of the abstract
requirements of ideal standards; it studied literature historically, and regarded it as necessarily determined in form and in matter through its direct
relation to the life of the people for whom and by
whom it was produced.   This conception of literature as an organic growth was one of the best gifts
of Herder to Goethe, and from their day to our
own it has been a commonplace of German literary
criticism.

It is not, then, because of the originality of his
fundamental principle that Taine's *History of*

English Literature is so important and significant
a book.   But nowhere else, unless in Scherer's
Geschichte der Deutschen Literatur, has the principle in question been applied so brilliantly for the
explanation of a whole national literature.   The
magnitude of the attempt, the importance of the
subject, and the brilliancy of the execution, have
insured the book a great vogue; and to-day, for
most English readers, Taine stands as the one
great representative of scientific method in the
study of literature.   Taine's work has done more
to popularize the conception of literature as the
direct and necessary expression of national life
than all the numberless tomes of conscientious
German philosophizing.

Then, again, Taine's theory, from its union of apparent simplicity and comprehensiveness, is always
at first sight enormously taking, and seems to
offer a perfect organon for the study of literature.
With characteristic love of clearness, precision,
and system, Taine tried to find a few ultimate
forces in terms of which to express all the infinitely various influences that shape and colour national life and determine its form and content.
The result of this effort was his adoption of the
now well-known categories, *race, moment,* and
milieu. The thoroughness and the skill with which
the influence of these ultimate forces is traced out
in all the minor groups of social facts, in religion,
philosophy, art, and science, are bound to be capti-

vating, particularly to young students who are
hungry for generalizations and eager to impose
themselves on the facts they handle.   Perhaps the
value of Taine's theory then depends fully as much
on its stimulating power as on any absolute certainty that can be claimed either for its subordinate principles or for the conclusions to which it
leads.

Attacks on the theory have from the first been
plentiful.   Among comparatively recent criticisms
that of M. Émile Hennequin in *La Critique scien-
tifique* is most interesting and suggestive.   M.
Hennequin appeared as a champion of "the great
man" in history and literature.   Under Taine's
treatment "the great man" seemed in danger of
being ruthlessly and prematurely resolved into his
elements; M. Hennequin was bent on rescuing him
and reconstituting him at any cost.   "The great
man," he insists, is not the product of his age; he
fashions his age in his own image.   He creates out
of nothing a beautiful ideal, either of action or of
passion, and imposes it on his sympathetic, impres-
sionable, but uncreative contemporaries.   He cannot be the mere product of his age, for both he and
his very opposite may exist under precisely the
same social conditions.   Goethe and Schiller belonged to one and the same nation in one and the
same age; so also with Hobbes and Milton, with
Byron and Crabbe, with Scott and Landor, and
with a host of other ill-mated couples, whom M.

Hennequin holds up to view for the bewilderment of the faithful followers of Taine. The great man, then, is not the product of his age, but is a mysterious original force, out of all explicable relation to his time, except as he brings his time under the spell of his genius.

It is, of course, not at all difficult to see how all this can be met from Taine's point of view; the criticism, though clever, is not damaging or convincing. But certain conclusions that M. Hennequin draws from this form of the great-man theory are interesting to the literary critic because of their practical applications.   Society, M. Hennequin insists, can properly be studied only through its typical great men, whose ideals dominate various social groups, and whose temperaments are their followers' temperaments intensified and magnified. Now, for the successful study of these typical temperaments, we must have, M. Hennequin urges, a thorough and elaborate system of psychological analysis, with points of view, methods, and terms which shall be used in common by all critics. This plea for coöperation among all critics in the thorough and systematic study of temperaments seems wholly in Taine's spirit, and suggests certain lines along which Taine's method can profitably be supplemented.

Such a scheme for the scientific study of the temperaments of authors, M. Hennequin, indeed, with a courage that may very well have come from

youth and inexperience, tried to outline. It is easy
for the ill-disposed to scoff at his elaborately determined points of view, at his ingenious terminology,
and at his formal schedules of facts and conclusions. But it is, nevertheless, perfectly plain that
some such scheme must be devised and put into
practice if criticism is ever to become a science, as
Taine and his followers have always been bent
upon making it. Moreover, Taine himself recognized this need with perfect distinctness. In the
eighth section of the introduction to his *History
of English Literature* he writes: "There is a particular system of inner impressions and operations
which makes an artist, a believer, a musician, a
painter, a man in a nomadic or social state; and of
each the birth and growth, the connection of ideas
and emotions, are different; each has his moral history and his special structure, with some govern-
ing disposition and some dominant feature. To
explain each, it would be necessary to write a
chapter of psychological analysis, and barely yet
has such a method been rudely sketched." This
passage may well enough have given M. Hennequin the first hint for his scheme of psychological
analysis.

Taine never for a moment claimed completeness
or finality for his method. He knew far better
than his assailants the difficulty of his problems,
and the necessary imperfections of any method
that can yet be devised for dealing with them.

But "his faith was large in time" and in the ultimate outcome of the coöperation of many ardent
students along the lines he had sketched. In 1866,
in his preface to *Essais de critique et d'histoire*,
he writes of the science of history: "Tel est le
champ qui lui est ouvert; il n'a pas de limites;
dans un pareil domaine, tous les efforts d'un
homme ne peuvent le porter en avant que d'un ou
deux pas; il observe un petit coin, puis un autre;
de temps en temps il s'arrête pour indiquer la voie
qui lui semble la plus courte et la plus sûre. C'est
tout ce que j'essaye de faire: le plus vif plaisir
d'un esprit qui travaille consiste dans la pensée du
travail que les autres feront plus tard." This passage contains the quintessence of Taine's spirit —
his generosity in appreciating the work of others,
his faith in the future, his indomitable energy,
and his enthusiastic devotion to the task in hand.
In his article on that prince of amateurs, Prosper
Mérimée, he says of the need of fixity of purpose
and of concentration: "Un homme ne produit tout
ce dont il est capable que lorsque, ayant conçu
quelque forme d'art, quelque méthode de science,
bref, quelque idée générale, il la trouve si belle
qu'il la préfère à tout, notamment à lui-même, et
l'adore comme une déesse qu'il est trop heureux de
servir." This fine singleness of purpose and stren-
uousness of pursuit characterizes all Taine's work
in literature. The great debt we owe to his scholarship and to his philosophic insight is too con-

stantly in our minds to need to find its way often into speech; but perhaps we are not so apt to realize how much he has done to redeem literary criticism from being a paltry juggling with fine phrases and to give it seriousness of purpose, dignity, and a recognized standing. He was charged with thorough-going materialism; but in an age of *décadence,* when the descendants of the Romanticists and idealists are for the most part engaged in dilettante experiments on their senses and emotions, such materialism as Taine's is as healthy as sea air. It is no wonder that when the death of M. Taine was announced, many students of literature felt as if they had lost a personal friend.

IMPRESSIONISM AND APPRECIA-
TION

PURE impressionism in literary criticism has of
late years grown into great favour, both among
critics themselves and with the public. The essentials of a good critic — so the rubric has come to
run — are sensitiveness to the varying appeal of
art, and the ability to translate this appeal into
images and phrases. The impressionist must have
delicacy of perception, mobility of mood, reverence
for the shade, and a sure instinct for the specific
integrating phrase, and for the image tinged with
feeling.

The popular legend that places Matthew Arnold
at the head of this critical tradition in England is
at least partly true; he certainly cared more for
the shade and sought more patiently to define it,
than any earlier English critic. The cult of the
shade was one of the many good things that came to
him from France. But Arnold the critic was no
match for Arnold the foe of Philistinism. Though
he had early insisted on the need of detachment in
literary criticism, Arnold suffered his moods to be
perturbed and his temperament to be blurred by

worry over practical and public questions of the
hour; and in later years he grew so intent on
coaching his fellow-countrymen in morals and
religion as to lose in some degree his critical zest
for refinements that had no direct ethical value.
It is rather to Walter Pater among English essay-
ists that the modern impressionist looks for precept
and example in his search for disinterestedness, for
artistic sincerity, and for flexibleness of temperament; and it is Pater who, more than all other
English critics, has illustrated what appreciative
criticism may accomplish.

Yet if we consider the matter more carefully,
impressionism is neither Arnold's nor Pater's
importation or invention. It is the result of far
deeper influences than any one man could have put
in play. It is indeed the expression in literature
of certain spiritual tendencies that have long been
developing, — tendencies the growth of which may
be traced in man's relation to nature as well as to
art. And it is because the moods and the instincts
and the methods of impressionism may thus be
discovered working themselves out connectedly
and progressively in the history of the human
spirit, that they must be regarded as justifying
themselves, and as deserving from even the most
conservative judges some degree of recognition and
acceptance. Little by little, during the last two
centuries, the human spirit has gained a finer and
closer sense of the worth and meaning of every

individual moment of pleasure in the presence alike
of nature and of art.   The record of this increase
of sensitiveness toward nature is to be found in
poetry, and toward art in criticism.

Thomson's *Seasons* may be taken as represent-
ing the utmost sensitiveness to nature of which
the early eighteenth century was capable.   Even
for a modern reader, Thomson's descriptions
still have considerable charm ; but what such
a reader soon notes is that the effects Thomson
portrays are all generalized effects, grouped significantly under the names of the four seasons.
Typical spring, typical summer, and so on —
these Thomson portrays, and of these he feels
what may be called the generalized emotional
value.   Beyond this typical treatment of nature and these generalized emotions he does
not pass.   As we go on, however, through the
poetry of the century, nature becomes gradually
more localized; poets dare to mark with specific
detail — to picture vividly — individual objects,
and they feel, and set down in their verse, the
general charm that *this* landscape, *this* smiling
valley, or *this* brimming river, has for an impres-
sionable observer.   Cowper has thus recorded much
of the beauty of the valley of the Ouse, with delicate truth and finished art.   Yet, be it noted, he
has included in his record little or no suggestion of
his own peculiar momentary moods.   In Wordsworth and the Romantic poets, the impressions

of nature are still further defined — are individual-
ized both in place and in time; at last we have
"the time and the place and the loved one all
together." Continually, in Romantic poetry, a
special bit of nature, tinged with the colour of a
fleeting mood, is enshrined in verse; the fusion
of nature with man's spirit is relatively complete.

In criticism, too, — that is, in man's conscious
relation to *art*, — a similar growth in sensitiveness
and in concreteness of matter and mood may be
traced. Addison was the first to try to work out,
in his *Pleasures of the Imagination*, the psychology
of artistic enjoyment; and his papers on *Paradise
Lost* come nearer being patient and vital appreciation of literature than any earlier English criticism
comes. Yet, after all, they get little beyond a
conventional and general classification of impressions. Addison's words of praise and blame are
few, literal, abstract, colourless. "Just," "natural," "elegant," "beautiful," "wonderfully beautiful and poetical" — these words and phrases, and
others like them, are used again and again; and
rarely indeed does Addison escape from such tag-
ging generalities, and define a personal impression
vividly and imaginatively. The history of literary
criticism from Addison's day to our own is, if
viewed in one way, the history of the ever-increas-
ing refinement of the critic's sensorium; it is the
history of the critic's increasing sensitiveness to

delicate shades of spiritual experience in his reaction on literature; and finally, it is the history of a growing tendency on the part of the critic to value, above all else, his own intimate personal relation to this or that piece of literature — a tendency that more and more takes the form of prizing the fleeting mood, the passing poignant moment of enjoyment in the presence of art, until at last certain modern critics refuse, on principle, to feel twice alike about the same poem.   In short, what has occurred is this: a poem in its relation to the critic has been gradually carried over from the outside world and made an intimate part of the critic's personality; it has been transformed from an external object, loosely related to universal mind and generalized emotion of which the critic stands as type, into a series of thought-waves and nerve-vibrations that run at a special moment through an active brain and a sensitive temperament.   For the pre-Addisonian critic, a poem was something to be scanned and handled, like an exquisite casket, and to be praised in general terms for its conventional design, its ingenious setting of jewel-like ornaments, and its sure and skilful execution; for the modern impressionistic critic, it is like the tone of a dear voice, like the breath of early morning, like any intangible greeting that steals across the nerves and cherishes them with an intimately personal appeal.

Impressionism, then, justifies itself historically.

P

But more than this, it justifies itself psychologically; for it recognizes with peculiar completeness the vitalizing power of literature — its fashion of putting into play the whole nature of each reader it addresses and its consequent, unlimited, *creative* energy. A piece of scientific writing offers to every man the same studiously unequivocal message; as far as the writer is consistently scientific, his terms have only an intellectual value, put only the mind into play, and guide all minds through the same routine of syllogism and inference to an inevitable conclusion. In contrast with this uniformity in the appeal of science is the infinite variableness and adaptability of literature. Every piece of literature is a mimic piece of life that tempts the reader to capture from it, with mind and heart and imagination, an individual bliss; he may, in some measure, shape it as he will — work out his own destiny with it. A theorem from Euclid once mastered is one and the same thing to every man — perennially monotonous. A play of Shakespeare's (or, for that matter, a sonnet of Rossetti's) speaks a language that varies in its power and suggestion according to the personality of the hearer, and even according to his mood; the poem gets its value, as life gets its value, from the temperament that confronts it; and it is this enchanting fickleness in literature that of late years impressionism has been more and more noting and illustrating, until some critics, like M. Anatole

France, assure us that literary criticism is nothing,
and should be nothing, but the recital of one's personal adventures with a book.

It is a mistake, then, to protest against the
growth of impressionism, as some nervous guar-
dians of the public literary conscience are inclined
to protest, as if a parasitic form of literature were
creeping into undue importance.   Regarded as literature about literature, impressionism may seem
an overrefined product—two degrees removed from
actual life, fantastically unreal; but regarded as the
intimate record of what a few happy moments have
meant to an alert mind and heart, impressionism is
transcendently close to fact.   The popularity of
impressionism is only one sign more that we are
learning to prize, above most things else, richness
of spiritual experience.   The sincere and significant mood — this is what we have come to care for,
whether the mood be suggested by life, by nature,
or by art and literature.   False moods expressed
maladroitly will doubtless try to get themselves
accepted, just as artificial poems about nature have
multiplied endlessly since Wordsworth's day.   The
counterfeit merely proves the worth of the original.
In an age that has learned to look on art with
conscious sincerity, and to recognize that the experience offered in art rivals religious experience in
renovating and stimulating power, there must more
and more come to be an imaginative literature that
takes its inspiration direct from art; of such

imaginative literature critical impressionistic writing is one of the most vital forms.

But though impressionistic writing may, as literature, not only justify itself, but prove to be sincerely expressive of some of the most original tendencies of the modern mind, the case is somewhat different when such writing is considered as literary criticism pure and simple, and is cross-questioned as to whether or no it can do the work that has hitherto been exacted of literary criticism.   Some French critic, perhaps M. Jules Lemaître, has been accused of turning an essay on a volume of Renan's *Histoire des origines du christianisme* into a lyrical recital of his own boyish delights with a Noah's ark.   Instances enough of such critical waywardness must have fallen under every one's eye who keeps the run of current essay-work.   Sainte-Beuve long ago said of Taine that in criticising an author he was apt to pull all the blankets to his own side of the bed.   And what was true of Taine, because of his devotion to theory, is true of many modern critics, because of their wilfulness and caprice — or, to put the matter more sympathetically, because of their over-ruling delight in their own sensibility and impressionableness ; they care for themselves more than for their author.   When such egoism goes with genius and with artistic resource, the resulting essays justify themselves, because they reveal in fascinating wise new phases of the ever-varying spiritual consciousness of the age. But even in such cases, where a really original personality, under the chance stimulus of literature, flashes out at us winning and imaginatively suggestive glimpses of itself, it may be doubted whether the essay that results is, properly speaking, criticism. Nor is this doubt a mere quibble over terms. The doubt involves several serious questions as regards the nature of a work of art and the critic's proper mode of approach to art. Paradoxical folk have sometimes asserted that what is best worth while in a work of art is what the author never meant to put in it, and that the superlative act of the critic is to find in a work of art for the delight of modern temperaments some previously unsuspected implication of beauty. Paradoxes aside, how much truth is there in this conception of the critic's task? and how much truth in the conception that goes with it of the essentially relative and variable character of art? We may grant that a piece of writing is *literature*, providing it is a beautiful and significant revelation of personality, whether the nerve-vibrations that it utters take their start from life or nature or art. But is such a piece of writing *criticism* if in commenting on a work of art it wilfully neglects its intended value as conceived in the mind of the original artist and as expressing, at least in part, the genius of the age whose life he shared? Can *criticism* properly neglect this original pleasure-value in a work of art? Can it furthermore neglect that permanent and deeply enwrought pleasure, involved in a work of art, through which it has always ministered and will always minister to normal human nature? Can *criticism* properly confine itself to the record of a momentary shiver across a single set of possibly degenerate nerves?

Surely, there is something objective in a work of art even when the work of art is regarded simply and solely as potential pleasure; and surely it is part of the task of the critic to take this objective character into full consideration. Unless he does so, his appreciation of the work will not be properly critical; nor indeed, for that matter, will his appreciation gather the full measure of personal delight that the work of art offers him. Just here lies the distinction between whimsical impressionism — which may be literature, very delightful literature, but lacks the perspective essential to criticism — and vital appreciation, which is indeed criticism in its purest and most suggestive form.

A work of art is a permanent incarnation of spiritual energy waiting for release. Milton long ago called a good book " the precious life-blood of a master-spirit stored up on purpose to a life beyond life." We nowadays may go even farther than this, and find treasured up in a piece of literature certain definite blisses and woes and flashes of insight that once went thrilling through a special temperament and mind. The most recent psychological explanations of artistic creation[1] concern themselves continually with the feelings of the artist; they trace out minutely the ways in which through the play of the artist's feelings a work of art is instinctively and surely generated. The poet concentrates his thought on some concrete piece of life, on some incident, character, or bit of personal experience; because of his emotional temperament, this concentration of interest stirs in him a quick play of feeling and prompts the swift concurrence of many images. Under the incitement of these feelings, and in accordance with laws of association that may at least in part be described, these images grow bright and clear, take definite shapes, fall into significant groupings, branch and ramify, and break into sparkling mimicry of the actual world of the senses — all the time delicately controlled by the poet's conscious purpose and so growing intellectually significant, but all the time, if the work of art is to be vital, impelled also in their alert weaving of patterns by the moods of the poet, by his fine instinctive sense of the emotional expressiveness of this or that image that lurks in the background of his consciousness. For this intricate web of images, tinged with his most intimate moods, the poet through his intuitive command of words finds an apt series of sound-symbols and records them with written characters.

[1] See, for example, Professor Dilthey's *Die Einbildungs-kraft des Dichters.*

And so a poem arises through an exquisite distilla-
tion of personal moods into imagery and into language, and is ready to offer to all future generations its undiminishing store of spiritual joy and
strength.

But it is not merely the poet's own spiritual
energy that goes into his poem. The spirit of the
age — if the poem include much of life in its scope,
if it be more than a lyric — enters also into the
poem, and moulds it and shapes it, and gives it in
part its colour and emotional cast and intellectual
quality. In every artist there is a definite mental
bias, a definite spiritual organization and play of
instincts, which results in large measure from the
common life of his day and generation, and which
represents this life — makes it potent — within the
individuality of the artist. This so-called " acquired
constitution of the life of the soul " — it has been
described by Professor Dilthey with noteworthy
acuteness and thoroughness — determines in some
measure the contents of the artist's mind, for it
determines his interests, and therefore the sensations and perceptions that he captures and auto-
matically stores up. It guides him in his
judgments of worth, in his instinctive likes and
dislikes as regards conduct and character, and con-
trols in large measure the play of his imagination
as he shapes the action of his drama or epic and
the destinies of his heroes. Its prejudices inter-
filtrate throughout the molecules of his entire

moral and mental life, and give to each image and idea some slight shade of attractiveness or repulsiveness, so that when the artist's spirit is at work under the stress of feeling, weaving into the fabric of a poem the competing images and ideas in his consciousness, certain ideas and images come more readily and others lag behind, and the resulting work of art gets a colour and an emotional tone and suggestions of value that subtly reflect the genius of the age. Thus it is that into a work of art there creeps a prevailing sort of spiritual energy that may be identified as also operating throughout the social life of the time, and as finding its further expressions in the precepts and the parables of the moralist, in the statecraft of the political leader, in the visionary dreams of the prophet and priest, and, in short, in all the various ideals, mental, moral, and social, that rule the age.

Now, as for the impressionistic writer about literature — he is apt to concern himself very little with this historical origin of a work of art. In dealing with the poetry of a long past age, he will very likely refuse the hard task of "trundling back his soul" two hundred or two thousand years and putting himself in close sympathy with the people of an earlier period. He is apt to take a poem very much as he would take a bit of nature — as a pretty play of sound or imagery upon the senses; and he may, indeed, capture through this half-sensuous treatment of art, a peculiar, though

wayward, delight.   But the appreciative critic is
not content with this.   He is, to be sure, well aware
that his final enjoyment of a poem of some earlier
age will be a far subtler and richer experience than
would be the mere repetition of the pleasures that
the poem gave its writer; that his enjoyment will
have countless overtones and undertones that could
not have existed for the producer of the poem or for
its original hearers.   But he also believes that the
generating pleasures that produced the work of
art, and that once thrilled in a single human spirit,
in response to the play and counter-play upon him
of the life of his time, must remain permanently
the central core of energy in the work of art; and
that only as he comes to know those pleasures with
fine intimacy, can he conjure out of the work of
art its perfect acclaim of delight for now and here.

Therefore the appreciative critic makes use of
the historical method in his study of literature.
He does not use this method as the man of science
uses it, for the final purpose of understanding and
explaining literature as a mass of sociological facts
governed by fixed laws.   This rationalization of
literature is not his chief concern, though he may
pass this way on his journey to his special goal.
But he is persuaded that in all the art and all the
literature that reach the present out of the past,
spirit speaks to spirit across a vast gulf of time;
that he can catch the precise quality of one of these
voices that come down the years only through the

aid of delicate imaginative sympathy with the life
of an elder generation; and that he can develop to
certainty of response this divining sympathy only
through patient and loyal study of the peculiar
play of the powers that built up in the minds and
the imaginations of those earlier men their special
vision of earth and heaven.

Difficult and elusive indeed are the questions he
must ask himself about the art from a distant age,
if he is to be sure of just the quality of the pleasure that went into its creation.   If it be Greek
art that he seeks to appreciate, he will study and
interpret it as the expression of the spirit of Greek
life, of a spirit that lived along the nerves and
fibres of an entire social organism, of a spirit that
sprung from the unconscious depths of instinct, out
of which slowly bodied themselves forth conscious
purposes and clear ideals, and that penetrated and
animated all fashions and forms of belief and behaviour, and gave them their colour and shape and
rhythm.   He will trace out and capture the quality
of this spirit as it expressed itself in the physical
life of the Greeks, in their social customs, in their
weaving of scientific systems, in their worship of
nature, and in the splendid intricacies of their religious ritual and mysteries.   And so he will hope
to gain at last a sure sense of the peculiar play of
energy that found release in some one of their
poems, or in the marble or bronze of a hero or a
god.

But the universal element in the poetry of an age by no means completes the objective character of the feeling the poetry has treasured for the delight of later times. In the case of all poetry not communal in its origin, the pleasure involved in a poem was generated in the consciousness of a single artist, and had a definite quality that partook of his individuality. Therefore the appreciative critic has a further nice series of identifications before him in his ideal search for the delight that inheres in a poem. Just what was the innermost nature of the poet who appeals to us in it, often so pathetically, down through the perilous ways of time? What was the special vision of life that he saw and felt the thrill of? What were the actual rhythms of the quicksilver passion in his veins? What was the honeydew on which he fed? What was the quintessential pleasure that he, among all men of his day, distilled into his verse?

Fantastic or insoluble these questions may seem unless with regard to poets about whom we have the closest personal memoranda. Yet critics have now and then answered such questions with surprising insight, even in the case of poets the gossip of whose lives is wholly unknown to us, and whose form of art was least personal in its revelations. Professor Dowden's grouping of Shakespeare's plays in accordance with the prevailing spiritual tone-colour of each and the moods toward life that are imaginatively uttered — moods of debonair light-heartedness, of rollicking jollity, of despairing pessimism, or of luminous golden-tempered comprehension — is an admirable example of the possible intimate interpretation of a poet's varying emotions as treasured in his art.

Here, then, are suggested two ways in which the appreciative critic who would make his impression of a work of art something more than a superficial momentary irritation of pleasure and pain will contrive to direct the play of his spiritual energy. He will realize, as far as he can, the primal vital impulse that wrought out the work of art; he will, in appreciating a poem, discover and recreate in his own soul the rhythms of delight with which the poem vibrated for the men of the age whose life the poem uttered; and he will also discern and realize those actual moods, those swift counter-changes of feeling, which once, in a definite place and at a definite moment, within the consciousness of a single artist evoked images and guided them into union, charged them with spiritual power, and called into rhythmical order sound-symbols to represent them thenceforth for ever.

But it must at once be noted that this mimetic enjoyment is after all only the beginning of that process of vitalization by which an appreciative critic wins from a work of art its entire store of delight.   The mood of the modern critic is something far subtler than any mere repetition of the mood of the original creative artist; it contains in itself a complexity and a richness of suggestion and *motifs* that correspond to all the gains the human spirit has made since the earlier age. Indeed, these subtle spiritual differences begin to declare themselves the moment the critic tries to describe the earlier enjoyment enshrined in a work of art. Walter Pater, for example, in noting in his essay on Winckelmann, the serene equipoise in Greek art between man's spirit and his body, at once involuntarily sets over against this mood the later mood in which spirit usurps and so tyrannizes over matter in its exaction of expression as to distort the forms of art, and render them "pathetic." No such contrast as this was present in the mind of the Greek as he enjoyed his own art; nor any contrast with a hungry, over-subtle intellectualism, such as nowadays makes the modern consciousness anxious for the individualizing accurate detail and the motley effects of realism. Yet these contrasts and others like them are part of the very essence of our modern delight in the freedom and largeness and calm strength of Greek art. Perhaps the Greek had more zest in his art than we have in it; but his enjoyment certainly had not the luxurious intricacy and the manifold implications of our enjoyment.

Always, then, in the complete appreciation of a work of art there is this superimposition of other moods upon the mood of the creative artist —

there is a reinforcement of the original effect by the delicate interfusion of new tones and strains of feeling.   Often this is as if harmonies once written for a harpsichord were played upon a modern piano whose " temperament " has been made rich and expressive through the artful use and adjustment of all possible overtones.   We shall be able to draw from the music new shades of meaning and of beauty.   But the original chords — those we should scrupulously repeat; and the original tone-colour, too, it were well to have at least in memory.   If a critic will win from early Florentine painting — from the work, for example, of Fra Lippo Lippi — its innermost value for the modern temperament, he will first recover imaginatively the sincere religious impulse and the naïve religious faith, as well as the dawning delight in the opening possibilities of a new art, which animated those early painters.   He will try to catch the very mood that underlies the tender mystic wistfulness of Lippo Lippi's Madonnas, and that gives them their soft and luminous constraint in the midst of the eager adoration of shepherd boys and attending angels.   He will recognize this mood as perhaps all the more appealing because of the quaint incompleteness of the artist's technique, his loyal archaic awkwardness, his religious formalism and symbolism, his unsure perspective, all the tantalizing difficulties of execution through which his vision of beauty made its way into colour and form. This mood will define itself for the critic through the aid of many nicely modulated contrasts — through contrast, it may be, with the more shadowed and poignantly mysterious Madonnas of Botticelli, and with the splendid and victorious womanhood of Titian's Madonnas, with the gentle and terrestrial grace of motherhood in those of Andrea del Sarto, and with the sweetly ordered comeliness of Van Dyck's Madonnas. But above all, it will define itself through contrast with our modern mood toward the Madonna and the religious ideas she symbolizes — through contrast with our sophisticated reverie, our hardly won half-credence, and our wise, pathetic insight. And through this contrast the earlier mood will gain for us a certain poignancy of delight; for the mood will come to us as something restored as by miracle out of the otherwise irrecoverable past of the spirit — out of the past of that spirit whose wayfaring through passions of aspiration and joy, and through drear times of sadness and desolation, was *our* wayfaring, since we have gathered into ourselves all the usufruct of it : —

"Oh ! what is this that knows the road I came,
   The flame turned cloud, the cloud returned to flame,
   The lifted, shifted steeps and all the way ? "

The appreciative critic, then, should know the characteristic joy of every generation of men, and the special joy of each individual artist. He is to

be a specialist in historic delight, as the poet is
a specialist in the joys of his own day and generation.   And therefore in trying to make real to
the men of his own time the special bliss that
an older work of art contains for them, the
appreciative critic will not be content, as is the
impressionistic critic, with interpreting it in terms
of some chance wayward mood.   He will wish to
relumine and make potent all that is emotionally
vital in the work of art; he will capture again its
original quality; he will revive imaginatively those
moments of bliss in the history of the human spirit
which are closely akin to this bliss and which yet
vary from it finely, and moments, too, that contrast broadly and picturesquely with it, all the
moments, indeed, which his divining instinct directs
him toward, as fit to throw into relief by contrast
what is quintessential in this one moment of spiritual ardour.   Thus he will try to offer to the men of
his own day a just appreciation of the peculiar joy
that, in the passage of years, the human spirit has
stored up for itself in this record of one of its
earlier phases of experience.

Throughout all his patient search for the precise
quality of a work of art, the critic will, of course,
make wise use of the science of æsthetics.   Its
analyses and principles are supposed to reveal and
sum up in terse formulas the mystery of beauty,
and they should therefore offer the critic a means
of steadying himself into a sincerely sympathetic

Q

and uneccentric report of the special charm that
lurks in a work of art.   Yet it must at once be
noted that for the appreciative critic the whole
region of æsthetics is full of danger.   Æsthetic
theorizing has been the pet pastime of many callous
and horny-eyed philosophers, whose only knowledge
of beauty has come by hearsay.   Nothing worse can
happen to a critic than to be caught in the meshes of
such thinkers' *a priori* theories, so much depends
on the critic's keeping an intimately vital relation
to the art of which he will interpret the peculiar
power.   Of recent years, however, the science of
æsthetics has been rescued from the region of
metaphysics, and has been brought very close to
fact and made very real and suggestive through
the use of psychological methods of study.   The
peculiar genius of the artist has been analyzed and
described; the characteristics of his temperament
have been noted with the nicest loyalty; and particularly the play of his special faculty, the imagination, as this faculty through the use of sensations
and images and moods and ideas creates a work of
art, has been followed out with the utmost delicacy
of observation by such acute and sensitive analysts
as M. Gabriel Séailles, M. Michaut, and Professor
Dilthey.   The behaviour, too, of the mind that is
enjoying a work of art — this has been minutely
studied and described; the "effects" and the "impressions" have been recorded by such masters of
silvery instruments for weighing a fancy and meas-

uring a motive as Fechner. The relations between all these impressions and effects and the form and content of a work of art have been tabulated. And so the science of æsthetics has become a really vital record of what may be called the mind's normal behaviour both in the creation and in the enjoyment of art.

The expert critic must some time or other have followed out all these devious analyses and tracked out the intricate workings both of the typical artist's and of the typical appreciator's mind. Such an abstract initiation will have quickened his powers of perception in numberless ways, will have made him alive to countless signs and suggestions in a work of art that might otherwise have appealed to him in vain, and above all will serve to steady him against extravagance and grotesque caprice in appreciation. In these analyses and principles he has the sensitive record of a consensus of expert opinion on the nature of artistic enjoyment — its causes and varieties. Through the help of these canons he may guard against meaningless egoism; he may manœuvre wisely within the region of the normal; he may keep within measurable distance of the tastes and the temperaments of his fellows. He will be able to test his impressions, to judge of their relative importance, to restrain personal whim within bounds, and to remain sanely true to the predominating interests of the normal human mind.

Not that the critic will let his use of æsthetic

formulas and points of view conventionalize or
stereotype his treatment of art. If he be happily
individual and alert, he will refuse to have forced
upon him a system, a method, unalterable precon-
ceptions, or habitual modes of approach to art. He
will keep in his repeated encounters with a work
of art much of the dilettante's bright wilfulness
and fickleness. He will go to it in all moods and
all weathers, will wait upon its good pleasure, and
will note delightedly all its fleeting aspects. But
these stray impressions will not content him, nor
will he care to report them as of themselves form-
ing a valid and final appreciation. He will play
the pedant with himself; he will, in sober moments
of wise hypocrisy, test the worth of his impressions by approved and academic standards; and he
will scrutinize them in the light of those canons
which the best modern theorizers in things æsthetic
have worked out psychologically. He will select
and arrange and make significant and unify. And
so, while approaching a work of art unconvention-
ally and communing with it intimately, he will, in
commenting on it, keep his casual and personal
sense of its charm within limits, and be intent on
doing full justice to what the work of art may well
mean to the normal man in normal moods.

Moreover, this æsthetic initiation will reveal to
the critic one special sort of pleasure stored in a
work of art that the layman is peculiarly apt to
miss — the pleasure that may be won from tracing

out the artist's mastery of technique and the secrets of his victorious execution. Here, again, the critic, if he is to make the work of art give up its quintessential quality, must call the historical method to his aid. An artist who, at any moment in the history of art, wishes to express his vision of beauty through the medium and the technique of his special art, whether it be painting, or music, or poetry, always confronts a definite set of limiting conditions. He finds certain fashions prevailing in his art; he finds in vogue certain conventional ways of treating material; he finds certain fixed forms offering themselves for his use — forms like the sonata and the concerto in music, or like the sonnet and the drama in poetry. These forms are traditional, have various laws and regulations attached to their handling, and in a sense limit the freedom of the artist, require him to make certain concessions, force him to conceive his material in stereotyped ways, and to cast it in predetermined moulds. An artist has always to find out for himself how far he can use these old forms; how far he can limit himself advantageously through accepting old conventions, whether his peculiar vision of beauty can be fully realized within the limits of the established technique, or whether he must be an innovator.

There is a curious and exquisite pleasure to be won from watching artists at close quarters with technical problems of this sort, and from observing the fine certainty with which genius gets the better of technical difficulties, through accepting a convention here, through following a fashion there, through slightly or even audaciously altering received forms or modes to secure scope for novel moods or hitherto unattained effects. An artist's vital relation to the past of his art — this is something that as it shows itself here and there in his work, the sensitive and alert critic finds keen pleasure in detecting. Here, again, the critic's specialized temperament and knowledge mediate between the art of earlier times and the men of his own day, and reveal through the help of æsthetics and history the peculiar pleasure with which art has, consciously or unconsciously, been charged.

Finally, the critic must bear in mind that it is distinctly for the men of his own day that he is revitalizing art; that it is for them that his specialized temperament is to use its resources. Every age, some one has said, must write its own literary criticism; and this holds specially true of appreciative criticism. The value of a work of art depends on what it finds in the consciousness to which it appeals; and because individuality is deeper and richer now than it has ever been before, and because the men of to-day are "the heirs of the ages," and have "ransacked the ages and spoiled the climes," a great traditional work of art ought to have a richer, more various, more

poignant value for modern men than it had for
their predecessors.   Even in the matter of sense-
perceptions this progress is noticeable.   "Our fore-
fathers," says a recent essayist on M. Claude Monet,
"saw fewer tones and colours than we; they had, in
fact, a simpler and more naïve vision; the modern
eye is being educated to distinguish a complexity
of shades and varieties of colour before unknown."
If there has been this increase of delicate power
even in a slowly changing physical organ, far
greater have been the increase and diversification
of sensitiveness in the region of spiritual perception.   New facts and ideas have been pouring into
the national consciousness from the physical sci-
ences during the last half-century, tending to trans-
form in countless subtle ways man's sense of his
own place in the universe, his ideals of brotherhood,
of justice, of happiness, and his orientation toward
the Unseen.   The half-mystical control that has of
late years been won over physical forces, the increased speed with which news flies from country
to country, the cheap and swift modes of travel
from land to land which break down the barriers
between the most widely divergent civilizations —
all these influences are reacting continually on the
life of the spirit, are stirring men's minds to new
thoughts and new moods, and developing in them
new aptitudes and new powers.   For minds thus
changed and thus touched into new alertness and
sensitiveness, past art must take on new phases,

reveal in itself new suggestions, and acquire or lose stimulating power in manifold ways. These alterations of value the appreciative critic ought to feel and transcribe.

And therefore the critic's must not be a "cloistered virtue"; at least imaginatively, he must be in sympathy with the whole life of his time. He must be intimately aware of its practical aims and preoccupations, of its material strivings, of all the busy play of its social activities, of its moral and religious perturbations, even of its political intrigues. Doubtless Matthew Arnold was right when he insisted on "detachment" as the first requisite of good criticism. But in urging detachment, Arnold meant simply that the critic must not let himself become the victim of practical problems or party organizations; that he must not let his imagination be seized upon by a set of definite ideas that are at once to be realized in fact; that he must not become an intellectual or moral or political bigot or a mere Tory or Radical advocate — the one-idea'd champion of a programme. The critic must have much of the dilettante's fine irresponsibility, perhaps even something of the cynic's amused aloofness from the keen competitions of daily life. But he must also have the dilettante's infinite variety, his intense dramatic curiosity, and his alert, wide-ranging vision. He should know the men of his own day through and through in all their tastes and tempers, and should be even more sensitively aware than they are themselves of their collective prejudices. So he should deepen his personality and as far as possible include within it whatever is most characteristic of his age. In the terms of all this, as well as of his own fleeting moods, he will try to appreciate past art. And so he will become, in very truth, the specialized temperament of the moment, interpreting the past to the present.

Continually, then, in his search for the pleasure involved in a work of art, the critic finds that he must go outside the work of art and go beyond his own momentary state of consciousness; he must see the work of art in its relations to larger and larger groups of facts; and he can charm out of it its true quality only by interpreting its sensations and images and rhythms as expressing something far greater than themselves, and as appealing to something far more permanent than his own fleeting moods. He must put the work of art in its historical setting; he must realize it in its psychological origin; he must conceive of it as one characteristic moment in the development of the human spirit, and in order thus to vitalize it he must be aware of it in its contrasting relations with other characteristic moments and phases of this development; and, finally, he must be alive to its worth as a delicately transparent illustration of æsthetic law. In regarding the work of art under all these aspects, his aim is primarily not to explain and not to judge or dogmatize, but to enjoy; to realize the manifold charm the work of art has gathered into itself from all sources, and to interpret this charm imaginatively to the men of his own day and generation.